A Free
and
Responsive
Press

A Free
and
Responsive
Press

The Twentieth Century Fund Task Force Report
for a NATIONAL NEWS COUNCIL

Background Paper by Alfred Balk

The Twentieth Century Fund/New York/1973

The Twentieth Century Fund, founded in 1919, and endowed by Edward A. Filene, devotes the major share of its resources to research, concentrating on objective and critical studies of major economic, political and social institutions. It usually publishes the results of its research in book form. The Fund attempts to ensure the scholarly quality of works appearing under its imprint; the Trustees and the staff, however, accord authors complete freedom in the statement of opinion and the interpretation of fact.

Library of Congress Catalog Card No. 72-97796
SBN 87078-129-4
Copyright © 1972 by The Twentieth Century Fund, Inc.
Manufactured in the United States of America

Foreword

As part of its research program on communications the Board of Trustees of The Twentieth Century Fund approved the setting up of a Task Force in 1971 to examine the feasibility of establishing a press council—or councils—in the United States. The Board did so because it was concerned about preserving the freedom of the press and improving its performance. These twin objectives, it felt, were vital to the public interest, and the public has lacked a means of expressing that interest. The Task Force was thus asked to consider the potential of a press council to fill this need.

The members of the Task Force, distinguished representatives of the public as well as professional journalists, who served in an individual capacity, had complete independence in undertaking this assignment. It was left to them to determine whether to recommend the establishment of a council. The Task Force debated at length about the need for a council and about what kind of council could best affirm and assert the public interest in a free press. Ultimately they recommended a new institution, national in scope, to serve both the press and the public.

In the course of its deliberations, the Task Force examined the councils established in other countries, notably in Britain. It also reviewed proposals for the creation of press councils in this country. In addition, it had the benefit of a report by Alfred Balk, the rapporteur for the Task Force, on existing councils in various parts of the United States. This research helped the Task Force to decide on the establishment of a national council whose primary focus would be on the national suppliers of news. The Task Force did not view such a council as eliminating the need for local, state, or regional councils. On the contrary, it recognized that there are flaws in press performance at the local level, and explicitly encouraged the formation of organizations to cope with local press coverage. But the Task Force believed that the establishment of a national model, concentrating on the most influential and professional news organizations, would enhance the value and viability of local efforts.

The national body proposed by the Task Force would not interfere with the press in the performance of its responsibilities. Indeed, the Task Force resolutely opposed any form of censorship or other impediment to freedom of expression. The members of the Task Force devoted considerable thought to the sanctions the council should be able to apply before coming to the realization that, as Justice Louis Dembitz Brandeis once observed, "sunlight is the most powerful disinfectant." The council would rely only on publicity to lend force to its findings.

As the Task Force conceived it, the council would emphasize the public stake in a free and independent press, a stake that the press cannot—and should not—defend single-handed. Independent of both the government and the craft of journalism, the council could report to the public both on the accuracy of news coverage and on threats, real and potential, against the freedom of the press to fulfill its responsibility of providing information to its readers and viewers.

The Twentieth Century Fund is grateful to all of the members of the Task Force for the time and effort they devoted to their task. As I was privileged to be present at most of their meetings, I can attest to the dedication and devotion of the entire group. The forging of a unanimous report called for give and take on all sides, but all of the Task Force members were united in their conviction that a national council is necessary. It is my hope that others will share that conviction.

M. J. Rossant, DIRECTOR
The Twentieth Century Fund
November 1972

Contents

Foreword   v

Members of the Task Force   viii

Report of the Task Force   1

Background Paper by Alfred Balk   11

    The Media under Attack   13
    Credibility   17
        Why the Gap?   17
        Narrowing the Gap   19
    The British Press Council   23
    Press Councils in America   31
    Minnesota's Press Council   37
    Honolulu's Community-Media Council   46
    What of the Future?   56
    Notes to Background Paper   63
    Bibliography   65

Appendices   67

    Constitution of the Minnesota Press Council   69
    Grievance Committee Precedural Rules,
    Minnesota Press Council (1971)   72
    Constitution of the British Press Council (1963)   80
    Organization of the Ontario Press Council   86

MEMBERS OF THE TASK FORCE

Barry Bingham, Sr.
Chairman of the Board
LOUISVILLE COURIER JOURNAL, Louisville, Kentucky

Lucy Wilson Benson
President
League of Women Voters, Washington, D.C.

Stimson Bullitt
President
KING BROADCASTING COMPANY, Seattle

Hodding Carter III
Editor
THE DELTA DEMOCRAT TIMES, Greenville, Mississippi

Robert Chandler
Editor
THE BULLETIN, Bend, Oregon

Ithiel de Sola Pool
Professor of Political Science
Massachusetts Institute of Technology, Cambridge, Massachusetts

Hartford N. Gunn, Jr.
President
PUBLIC BROADCASTING SYSTEM, Washington, D.C.

Richard Harwood
Assistant Managing Editor
THE WASHINGTON POST, Washington, D.C.

Louis Martin
Editor
CHICAGO DEFENDER, Chicago

John B. Oakes
Editorial Page Editor
THE NEW YORK TIMES, New York City

C. Donald Peterson
Justice of the Minnesota Supreme Court, St. Paul, Minnesota

Paul Reardon
Associate Justice of the Supreme Judicial Court, Boston

Richard Salant
President
CBS NEWS, New York City

Jesse Unruh
Los Angeles

REPORT OF THE TASK FORCE

The United States is now passing through an era marked by divisive, often bitter, social conflict. New groups have coalesced to assault the privileges of the established; new ideas have arisen to challenge the validity of the old. Stridency and partisanship, militancy and defiance are in the air.

Reporting the news has always meant telling people things they may not want to hear. In times of social conflict, this task is all the more difficult. Skepticism turns to cynicism. Detachment is too often perceived as hostility. The clamor to "tell it like it is" too often carries with it the threat to "tell it like we see it, or else." The Greeks were not alone in wanting to condemn the bearer of bad tidings.

Disaffection with existing institutions, prevalent in every sector of society, has spread to the media of public information—newspapers and magazines, radio and television. Their accuracy, fairness, and responsibility have come under challenge. The media have found their credibility questioned, their freedom threatened, by public officials whose own credibility depends on the very media they attack and by citizens whose own freedom depends on the very institutions they threaten.

A free society cannot endure without a free press, and the freedom of the press ultimately rests on public understanding of, and trust in, its work.

The public as well as the press has a vital interest in enhancing the credibility of the media and in protecting their freedom of expression. One barrier to credibility is the absence in this country of any established national and independent mechanism for hearing complaints about the media or for examining issues concerning freedom of the press. Accordingly, this Task Force proposes:

That an independent and private national news council be established to receive, to examine, and to report on complaints concerning the accuracy and fairness of news reporting in the United States, as well as to initiate studies and report on issues involving the freedom of the press. The council shall limit its investigations to the principal national suppliers of news—the major wire services, the largest "supplemental" news services, the national weekly news magazines, national newspaper syndicates, national daily newspapers, and the nationwide broadcasting networks.

As a result of economic changes and technological advances, these few giant news organizations, with their unprecedented news gathering resources, now provide the majority of Americans with most of their national and international news. The Associated Press and United Press International, the two principal wire services, supply material to 99 percent of all daily newspapers as well as to most radio and television stations. Complementing these facilities are the major nationwide radio-television networks, the national weekly news magazines, national newspaper syndicates, nationwide daily newspapers (the *Wall Street Journal* and the *Christian Science Monitor*), and the "supplemental" news services, increasingly comprehensive wire services sold to large and small newspapers by organizations such as *The New York Times* and, jointly, *The Washington Post* and *The Los Angeles Times.*

This concentration of nationwide news organizations—like other large institutions—has grown increasingly remote from and unresponsive to the popular constituencies on which they depend and which depend on them. The national media council proposed by this Task Force will serve its purpose most effectively by focusing on the major national suppliers.

Publishers and broadcasters are justifiably suspicious of any proposal—no matter how well intended—that might compromise editorial independence, appear to substitute an outsider's judgment for that of responsible editors, ensnare newsmen in time-consuming explanations, or lend itself to the long-term undermining of press freedom. The press of the United States is among the best in the world and still improving, but it fails to meet some of the standards of its critics, among them, journalists. Moreover, a democratic society has a legitimate and fundamental interest in the quality of information available to it. Until now, the citizen who was without benefit of special office, organization, or resources had no place to bring his complaints. Until now, neither the public nor the national news media have been able to obtain detached and independent appraisals when fairness and representativeness were questioned. The proposed council is intended to provide this recourse for both the public and the media.

The Council is not a panacea for the ills of the press or a court weighing complaints about the responsibility of the press. With its limited scope and lack of coercive power, the Council will merely provide an independent forum for public and press discussion of important issues affecting the flow of information.

Editors and publishers may fear that a media council will stimulate public hostility; some even suspect that it might curtail rather than preserve their freedom. The core of the media council idea, however, is the effort to make press freedom more secure by providing an independent forum for debate about media responsibility and performance, so that such debate need not take place in government hearing rooms or on the political campaign trail. The Task Force unanimously believes that government should not be involved in the evaluation of press practices. The Task Force also recognizes that there is concern about the relationship of press council procedures to the confidentiality of news sources. It is convinced that the founders must address themselves to the issue of confidentiality in the charter and the Council must respect and uphold essential First Amendment rights by maintaining confidentiality of news sources and of material gathered in news production in its proceedings.*

The idea of a national council is not new. Sweden and Great Britain have had press councils for many years and one recently was set up in New Zealand. Britain's council, composed of private citizens and journalists, most closely resembles what the Task Force proposes.† Although the British council has not achieved all of its objectives in the past decade it has won substantial acceptance.

---

*Hereafter asterisk indicates point on which Richard Salant abstains.

†Immediately after World War II, Britain was shaken by political and social dissonance similar to that of the United States today. Press mergers, closings, and allegations of sensationalism and slanting of news generated public concern and debate in and out of Parliament. The result of this debate was a Royal Commission investigation. The report of the commission recommended, among other measures, the creation of a private press council, to hear and act on complaints about the press and to speak in defense of press freedom when appropriate. Broadcasting (then only the government-sponsored BBC) was excluded from the recommendation.

Newspaper proprietors deliberated at length and delayed action for months; then agreed to a council with no public members. In 1963, after further Parliamentary threats and another Royal Commission report, the present successful citizen-journalist council was established.

Twenty of the Council's twenty-five members are chosen by eight publisher and journalistic staff organizations; the remaining five are public members elected for fixed terms by the Council. The chairman is also a public member. (Lord Devlin, one of Britain's most prominent judges was the Council's first public chairman). The secretariat is composed of three professional journalists. The Council's only power lies in the publicity given its findings. Its expenses—slightly more than $70,000 a year—are borne entirely by national press organizations.

"Foreigners who study the British Press Council usually come away in a mixed mood of admiration and bafflement," according to Vincent S. Jones, former executive editor of the Gannet Newspaper Editors. "It ought not to work, they feel, but somehow it does."

In the United States, a number of communities and one state—Minnesota—have in recent years established press councils. Some are no longer active; all appear to have been constructive regardless of their longevity, and experience has brought increasing accomplishment and decreasing mortality.

Significantly, the most recent and ambitious undertaking, Minnesota's, was initiated by a newspaper association. This development suggests that, as in Britain, opposition may be converted to neutrality and even support, as experience and objective observation dispel myths about the aims and operations of press councils.

Although the American Society of Newspaper Editors and other associations have failed to implement proposals for journalistic "ethics" or "grievance" machinery, investigations by this Task Force indicate that a substantial number of editors, publishers, and broadcasters will participate in a council experiment. As an editorial in the November 28, 1970, issue of *Editor and Publisher* observed: "Newspaper editors and publishers will never stand in the way of organizing such councils, but very few of them will be prime movers in setting them up."

The most frequently advanced proposal—a comprehensive nationwide press council on the British model—is impractical, if not undesirable, in the United States. The vastness and regional diversity of the United States, the number of individual publications and broadcasting stations, and problems of logistics and expense all militate against the formation of a comprehensive nationwide council. The weighing of one journalistic practice in New England against another in Arizona would present an impossible task. Nevertheless, individual newspapers and radio-television stations may find it useful to participate in regional, state, or local councils that are either now in existence or yet to be formed. This Task Force encourages the establishment of such councils. Several authorities have suggested that if such a comprehensive council eventually is formed, it will most likely evolve "from the ground up," possibly as a federation of local or regional councils. We urge that such councils be formed.

Accordingly, the Task Force makes the following recommendations for the establishment of a national council:

1. The body shall be called the Council on Press Responsibility and Press Freedom.
2. The Council's function shall be to receive, to examine, and to report on complaints concerning the accuracy and

fairness of news coverage in the United States as well as to study and to report on issues involving freedom of the press. The Council shall limit its review to news reporting by the principal national suppliers of news. Specifically identified editorial comment is excluded.

3. The principal national suppliers of news shall be defined as the nationwide wire services, the major "supplemental" wire services, the national weekly news magazines, national newspaper syndicates, national daily newspapers, nationwide commercial and noncommercial broadcast networks.

4. The Council shall consist of fifteen members, drawn from both the public and the journalism profession, but always with a public chairman. Both print and broadcast media shall be represented. No member shall be affiliated with the principal nationwide suppliers of news.*

5. A grievance committee, a subcommittee of the Council, will meet between eight and twelve times a year to screen public complaints. When appropriate, the committee and Council staff will engage teams of experts to investigate complaints.

6. The Council shall meet regularly and at such special meetings as shall be required. Its findings shall be released to the public in reports and press releases. Routine activities will be handled by a permanent staff, consisting of an Executive Director and professional assistants. The Executive Director should have significant journalistic experience.

7. Complaints about coverage by the designated national suppliers of news shall be handled according to procedures similar to those of the British and Minnesota press councils. Thus, the procedures will include a requirement that any complainant try to resolve his grievance with the media organization involved before the Council may initiate action on a complaint. Complainants will be required to waive the right to legal proceedings in court on any matter taken up in Council proceedings.

   It is expected that most complaints will be settled without recourse to formal Council action.*

8. Individuals and organizations may bring complaints to the Council. The Council may initiate inquiry into any situation where governmental action threatens freedom of the press.

9. Action by the Council will be limited to the public reporting of Council decisions. The Council will have no enforcement powers.

10. Where extensive field investigation is required, the Council may appoint fact-finding task forces.

11. The Council's executive offices shall be at a location designated by its members. Regardless of the ultimate location, the Council shall consider emphasizing its national character by scheduling at least some meetings on a rotating basis throughout the country.

12. The Task Force shall appoint a founding committee which will select the Council's original members, incorporate the Council, adopt its constitution, and establish the initial budget.

13. Terms of office shall be three years (with terms of charter members to be staggered on the basis of a drawing of lots); members shall be limited to two consecutive terms. Members must resign from the Council if they leave the vocational category which was the basis for their selection. On retirement of a Council member, the Council shall appoint a nominating committee made up of representatives from foundations, the media, and the public. The Council shall make the final selection from the choices presented to it.

14. The founding committee shall incorporate the Council and establish the initial budget for a minimum of three to six years. It is suggested that the annual budget will be approximately $400,000.*

15. The Task Force appoints Justice Roger Traynor, former chief justice of California, head of the founding committee and chairman of the Council.

16. The Council's processes, findings, and conclusions should not be employed by government agencies, specifically the Federal Communications Commission, in its decisions on broadcast license renewals. Failure to observe this recommendation would discourage broadcasters from supporting or cooperating with the Council.

The national media council proposed here will not resolve all the problems facing the print and broadcast media, nor will it answer all of the criticisms voiced by the public and by the politicians. It will, however, be an independent body to which the public can take its complaints about press coverage. It will act as a strong defender of press freedom. It will attempt to make the media accountable to the public and to lessen the tensions between the press and the government.

Any independent mechanism that might contribute to better public understanding of the media and that will foster accurate and fair reporting and public accountability of the press must not be discouraged or ignored. The national media council is one such mechanism that must be established now.

**BACKGROUND PAPER
BY ALFRED BALK**

The Media under Attack

The 1960s were a decade of harsh discovery for Americans—discovery that social and governmental institutions, long taken for granted, no longer responded adequately to the needs and demands of a society under stress. And the nation's newspapers, news magazines, television, and radio—the media that communicated the assaults on established values and beliefs to the American public—found that they themselves had become targets of mounting accusation.

The press and broadcasting have never been beyond criticism, nor should they be. But there is abundant evidence that the criticism they now draw differs significantly in degree and kind from that of earlier periods.

One indication is the frequency and zeal with which the nation's highest public officials disparage the news media. Concurrently the government has taken a series of actions which would have been unthinkable a decade ago: "blanket" subpoenas of journalists' notes, photographs, and film and videotape "outtakes"; phone calls and letters to media executives from White House officials and the chairman of the Federal Communications Commission to inquire into planned or already disseminated comment; and, perhaps most dramatic, the Justice Department effort in the Pentagon Papers case to censor by prior restraint some of the nation's oldest and most respected newspapers.

There are other signs of disaffection. Criticism of the press has been the harshest in years—some of it the vulgar poison from racist and ethnic prejudice that editors recognize as symptomatic of deep frustration and often dangerous discontent. After two of Vice-president Agnew's attacks on the media, Norman E. Isaacs, then president of the American Society of Newspaper Editors, reported a flood of "vicious" and "venomous" remarks; Robert Donovan of *The Los Angeles Times* noted that "yahoos are telephoning obscenities to television stations." The situation described by Ken Berg, editor of the Mankato, Minnesota, *Free Press*, probably is typical of that in many communities: "I'm getting twice the volume of mail I used to get, a lot of it from people who used to keep silent but are secretly pleased to see the media taking a licking."

United States Senator Jack Miller of Iowa told a New York County Lawyers Association in 1971 that in his opinion journalists should be licensed, with each subject to "having his privilege . . . to practice his profession revoked for unethical conduct." Dr. Walter W. Menninger expressed similar sentiments in a 1970 speech to the National Press Club in Washington. Government-sponsored "watchdog" councils have been proposed (though the proposals have not been acted upon) in both the Washington and Minnesota legislatures, among others; and at the 1970 Iowa American Legion convention a resolution called for a federal agency to deal with complaints against the press. The proposal ultimately was amended to request a media-established complaints agency.

Growing concern is being expressed about the difficulties of gaining access to newspaper columns or broadcast time—to the point that some legal theorists assert that a "right of access" to communications media exists and should be defined. In 1967, Jerome A. Barron, a professor at the George Washington University Law School, urged in a *Harvard Law Review* article an "interpretation of the First Amendment . . . focused on the idea that restraining the hand of government is quite useless in assuring free speech if a restraint on access is effectively secured by private groups." Not long afterwards, United States Representative Farbstein of New York introduced bills to require newspapers to present conflicting views on issues of public importance and to empower the Federal Communications Commission to enforce the Fairness Doctrine on newspapers. Another bill, introduced in 1970 by Representative Michael Feighan of Ohio, would require newspapers to print all advertisements submitted and create a right of reply for any organization or individual that has been the subject of editorial comment by a newspaper.

In addition, citizen organizations have sprung up to monitor media performance, challenge media practices in hiring of minority groups and related matters, and in some instances, to contest the renewal of local broadcast franchises.[1]

These developments scarcely have passed unnoticed by the nation's newsmen. Katharine Graham, president of the Washington Post Company, told a Southern California Distinguished Achievement Awards Dinner in 1969:

> The American people do not seem at all happy with their press. The fact itself . . . is beyond dispute and the nation's publishers are acutely aware of the general indictment. . . . It would be easy—and I think it would be foolish—to try to minimize the importance of this critical clamor. . . . All . . . in so large a chorus are hardly likely to be wrong.

And the Associated Press Managing Editors' publication, *APME News*, stated in August 1969 that "a 'credibility gap exists' for the press without question. . . . This is widely acknowledged both by editors and by public officials replying to a questionnaire."

Other observers tend to agree. A 1970 staff report for the National Commission on the Causes and Prevention of Violence declared:

> [The press] . . . has improved immeasurably since the beginning of the century. But the changes in American society have been more than measurable; they have been radical. . . . A crisis of confidence exists today between the American people and their news media.

However, the extent to which the public has lost confidence in the news media may have been exaggerated. In June 1971, for example, public opinion pollster Louis Harris wrote:

> Much of the alleged public unhappiness with news coverage in newspapers and on television appears to be overstated by critics of the media. Charges ranging from the news media being "too liberal" to "too conservative" as well as "too full of violence" or "too easy on protesters" simply have not gained majority acceptance among the readers and viewers themselves.

Even so, the time has clearly come to reexamine the dynamics of journalism in the United States today. How valid are the assumptions on which the media now operate? What is the relationship between these assumptions and the way in which the job of communicating is being done? In what ways is media performance failing to respond to the pressures of a changing society? What can be done to improve that performance and thereby strengthen the confidence of the public in the communications media?

One of the innovations most frequently suggested is a press, or media, council—a citizen-journalist group which, among other functions, could receive and act on specific complaints about news media performance and also defend freedom of the press. Such councils could be organized on a local, regional, or national basis. They have been established in Europe, and significant experiments with them already are under way in this country.

The purpose of this paper is to try to penetrate the mist that has enveloped the press council idea, to report on the British and American experiments, and to consider what relevance the press council may have to American media performance lags and credibility problems.

Credibility

Why the Gap?

To understand American news media credibility problems, one must first understand that a credibility "gap" is not peculiar to the news media. Government, business, labor, universities, churches—many times seem to have a gap between expectations and performance. Columnist David Broder observed in the *Washington Monthly*, "The press is caught up in what John Gardner has called the crisis of our times—the necessity for institutional adaptation to the forces of change."

Some believe the media are trapped by an archaic concept of their mission. As Max Ways wrote in *Fortune* in October 1969:

> Conditioned by its own past, journalism often acts as if its main task were still to report the exceptional and dramatically different against a background of what everybody knows. . . . Much of journalism still operates as if its circulation and its usefulness depended on the second hand of the clock rather than the depth of perception, the accuracy of its report, the relevance of its coverage, and the balance of its judgment.

At a time when in-depth reporting is required, broadcasting—from which most Americans say they obtain their news—offers flashy headlines and sketchy film clips. The networks and very large broadcasting stations have self-trained and independent news staffs, but most stations remain the "rip and read" variety, weaving items from wire services and local newspapers into what they characterize as local news coverage.

Journalism, as one observer noted, is "a profession grafted onto an industry." Its professional functions of writing and editing—like those of law, medicine, and engineering—require a high degree of education and experience, yet there are no nationwide standards of training, performance, and ethical practices, and the editorial function is only one component of print media operations (and an even smaller one in broadcasting). The editor, as chief journalistic "officer" in a corporate enterprise, therefore, is very likely to lack ultimate responsibility for ethical and procedural practices, unless he happens also to be the publisher or, in the case of broadcasting, the station owner. These positions are usually occupied by businessmen.

Newspaper newsrooms, meanwhile, except for the absence of cuspidors, in many ways look and operate much as they did early in the century. Because of union obstructionism or management penury or both, newspapers as an industry in the past half-century have embraced fewer technological changes than almost any other business but the U.S. Post Office. Pay and working conditions in journalistic organizations vary enormously, but in general, journalistic skills command smaller rewards than sales or other business skills.

Printing and publishing once were modestly financed storefront operations, and keen competition was the rule. Today both newspaper and broadcasting enterprises tend to be big—or at least moderately big—business. Nearly half of U.S. daily newspapers, representing some three-fifths of daily and Sunday circulation, are owned by newspaper groups and chains, including diversified business conglomerates. One-newspaper towns have become the rule, with effective competition operating in only 4 percent of our large cities.

Broadcasting operations have become concentrated in fewer and fewer hands, resulting in what Yale University President Kingman Brewster has called a "closed loop."

> Politicians must raise money from corporations in order to pay the network's enormous cost of television time. Corporate advertisers call the network tune. And the networks must curry favor with the successful politicians to assure their franchise.

Moreover, the major sources of national and international news are largely limited to the giant wire services of the Associated Press, United Press International, and several supplementary services. This quasi-monopoly of sources imposes limits on the selection of news, the diversity of items made available to the public, and their editorial content and viewpoint.

The relatively small proportion of time allocated by broadcasters to news and public affairs intensifies the effects of these limitations in broadcasting, particularly in television. In some instances, community or area publishing and broadcasting operations are in the hands of a single proprietor who may fail not only to provide diversity of news and opinion and access to the news forum but even to apply standards of fairness and accuracy generally assumed to be the minimum sanctioned by American journalism.

Narrowing the Gap

From the adequacy of recruitment and training of journalists to the definitions of "news," the philosophy and practice of journalism now are being intensely debated, both inside and outside the journalistic community. Among the more notable external developments are:

The birth of about a dozen local journalism reviews. At this writing they are published in Anchorage; Houston; Los Angeles; Baltimore; Chicago; New York City; Philadelphia; Providence, Rhode Island; Holyoke, Massachusetts; St. Louis; Minneapolis-St. Paul; Denver; Long Beach, California; and Honolulu. Of varying quality, they provide an outlet for analysis and criticism of local media, in many cases by staff members of the media being criticized.

The rise of "city magazines" and underground newspapers. Like local journalism reviews, they provide outlets—also of varying quality—for "alternate" views of contemporary issues, as well as for critiques of the performance of the major news media.

Citizen organizations to improve broadcasting. The Office of Communication of the United Church of Christ, directed by the Reverend Everett C. Parker, has successfully challenged questionable media practices in Mississippi, Texas, Arkansas, Washington, and elsewhere. Other groups such as the National Citizens Committee for Broadcasting, Action for Children's Television, and Black Efforts for Soul in Television have formed citizen lobbies to influence programming standards, advertising practices, and employment policies.

It is instructive to consider *the truth-in-advertising movement,* in relation to the media credibility issue. Spurred by Ralph Nader's Center for the Study of Responsive Law and several consumer groups, the Federal Trade Commission has created new government standards for advertising acceptability; and, in 1971, the advertising industry itself set up a National Advertising Review Board. The F.T.C. now requires that advertisers be able to prove claims made in advertising, and the Federal Communications Commission has ruled that under the Fairness Doctrine it can order granting of time for replies to commercials on the environment, auto safety, and the like. The National Advertising Review Board, with former Ambassador Charles W. Yost as chairman, receives complaints from consumers who believe they have been misled by advertising; hears witnesses; requests corrective action by advertisers found in violation of its standards; and, as a final step, when necessary, turns its findings over to the appropriate government agency and publicizes its action.

American journalism for the past decade has been undergoing increasingly intensive self-examination. As a result, the field is increasingly susceptible to redirection. Already, significant changes in the journalistic landscape have occurred. These include:

The "reporter power" movement. In contrast to earlier years, when reporters simply accepted supervisors' or management edicts without formal discussion, reporters at some newspapers have requested at least a consultative role in matters of professional policy. A few organizations have responded by encouraging the dialogue. These include the *Wall Street Journal,* Chicago *Sun-Times,* Minneapolis *Tribune,* Philadelphia *Bulletin,* and *Newsweek.* At the Burlington, Iowa, *Hawk-eye,* reporters elect the managing editors, and at the Minneapolis *Tribune,* reporters as a group have veto power over selection of assistant city editors.

New "feedback" mechanisms in newspapers. These include expanded letters-to-the-editor columns, Opposite-Editorial (Op Ed) pages open to nonstaff writers, and special columns by editors discussing media practices. While *The New York Times* Op Ed page is perhaps the most influential of its *genre,* notable examples also exist in Milwaukee, Tucson, and smaller cities. *The Milwaukee Journal* features a regular Op Ed column ("In My Opinion") to which outsiders contribute, and *The Salt Lake City Tribune* not only opens a column called "Common Carrier" to outsiders, but pays a five-member community panel (an educator, a labor leader, an environmental engineer, a former League of Women Voters official, and a Chicano government employee) to screen copy for it. Reader questions and complaints about the media are the subject of columns in *The Cleveland Press* ("We're Listening"); Utica, New York, *Observer-Dispatch* ("Observations"); St. Paul, Minnesota, *Pioneer-Press* ("The Editor's Notebook"); Easton, Pennsylvania, *Express* ("Express Yourself"); and other newspapers.

"Ombudsmen" and house critics. In Sweden, where the office of Parliamentary Ombudsman long has existed to mediate citizen problems with government, the Newspaper Publishers Association in 1969 decided to augment the nation's half-century-old press council with a Press Ombudsman. Nominated by the Parliamentary Ombudsman, the president of the National Bar Association, and the chairman of a joint press group called the Committee for Press Cooperation, the Press Ombudsman independently investigates complaints against the press and has the authority to refer cases to the press council. Although no such office exists in the United States, several newspapers have designated senior editors to be ombudsmen, and the practice appears to be spreading.

The *Courier-Journal* and *Times* in Louisville inaugurated the practice in this country in 1967 after A. H. Raskin of *The New York Times* wrote an article in *The New York Times* Magazine of June 11, 1967, titled "What's Wrong with American Newspapers." In it he bemoaned the lack of internal criticism in newspapers and urged a department headed by a person with sufficient authority to "serve as an ombudsman for the readers, armed with authority to get something done about valid complaints and to propose methods for more effective performance of all the paper's services to the community." Norman E. Isaacs, then editor of the Louisville papers, responded to the idea immediately, designating as full-time ombudsman long-time *Courier-Journal* city editor John Herchenroeder.

Representatives of more than two dozen newspapers have written or visited Louisville to learn about Herchenroeder's job, and several now have in-house ombudsmen. They include the St. Petersburg, Florida, *Times* and *Evening Independent*, where former managing editor Del Marth writes "The People's Voice" column, and the Lafayette, Indiana, *Journal* and *Courier*, where associate editor Paul James writes the "Help" column. In a variation of this, the Minneapolis *Star* and *Tribune* operate separate complaint-investigation departments: the Bureau of Accuracy and Fair Play (a title originated by Joseph Pulitzer at the old New York *World*) at the *Tribune*; Reader's Referee at the *Star*. In both instances, a senior staff member investigates complaints and selects stories at random to be checked by sending questionnaires to persons mentioned in them. Corrections and letters of clarification are published as recommended, and the *Star*'s editor discusses media problems in a column titled "Old Ref."

Since 1970, *The Washington Post* has experimented with still another variation on the ombudsman—a "house critic." To guard against what the *Post* owner Katharine Graham described as "creeping bias, laziness, inaccuracy, and the sins of omission," the ombudsman, or house critic, checks each day's paper for fairness, balance, and accuracy, critiques coverage in memos to the editor; and discusses these and related matters in periodic columns titled "The News Business." Richard Harwood, now the *Post*'s national news editor, was the paper's first house critic. He was followed by former assistant managing editor Ben Bagdikian. Now the position is held by veteran black reporter Robert C. Maynard.

Fair Trial/Free Press Committees. Since the Warren Commission in 1964 urged cooperation to reduce prejudicial publicity surrounding court proceedings, bar associations and the news media in some three-dozen states have formed joint committees to confront the problem. The result—joint guidelines or statements of principles in about half of the states—represents precedent-setting cooperative endeavor. Although this is only a start, willingness to discuss press practices with an outside interest group reveals a significant shift in media conceptions of self-interest. It is in this context that rising interest in media councils should be viewed.

The British Press Council

More than a half-dozen European countries—Sweden, Switzerland, West Germany, Italy, and Britain among them—have press councils, but Britain's probably is the most famous. It also is of the most interest to the United States, because of the similarity of British and U. S. societies, the kinship of the presses of the two countries, and the circumstances out of which the British Press Council grew.

Unlike the United States, Britain is small enough to be dominated by a few national newspapers with circulations exceeding all but a few local newspapers in the United States, and there are only two national broadcasting organizations: the government-financed, noncommercial BBC (British Broadcasting Corporation) and the commercial ITA (Independent Television Authority). Publications display greater extremes of taste, from the staid *Times* of London to flamboyant tabloids reminiscent of American "yellow journalism" of the twenties and thirties. Media standards, concentration of ownership, and the demise of major publications have been especially sensitive issues in Britain. In the period since World War II, the aftereffects of wartime economic controls, competition from television for readers' attention, rising education levels, and the strains rooted in Britain's decline as a world power all tended to focus attention on the news media.

Political stresses were another factor. Big-business ownership, in Britain and elsewhere, tends toward the politically conservative. With the rise to power of Clement Attlee's Labor Government, prominent members of the Socialist wing objected both to alleged sensationalism in the press and to its treatment of economic and political issues. This, combined with anxiety about economic problems of the press, prompted the National Union of Journalists to urge that a Royal Commission study the field. In introducing the bill authorizing the Commission, Haydn Davis, a Labor party MP and journalist, said:

> This motion has nothing at all to do with the so-called sensitiveness of the Front Bench or the prima donna temperament of any politicians. It is based on a resolution passed by journalists because they believe in the freedom of the press. . . . We have watched the destruction of great newspapers. We have watched the combines come in, buying up and killing independent journals, and we have seen the honorable profession of journalism degraded by high finance and big business. . . . The central issue is this. Can we or can we not have real freedom of the press in a system of combines and chain newspapers?

There was lengthy and sometimes rancorous debate.

"The acceptance of the request for an inquiry will create doubt and suspicions in the minds of the public here at home as to the essential integrity of the press," said Major Sir David Maxwell Fyfe, Conservative MP, "and still more it will arouse dangerous suspicions in other countries. What is really behind this motion is not freedom of expression at all; honorable members want to saddle the country with a number of papers of their own way of thinking."

Max Aitken, MP and general manager of the *Sunday Express*, argued that a Royal Commission would waste the time of editors and public officials, as well as public money, because the Commission would not find anything new; that papers already give such "free expression of opinion" that the *Sunday Express* and the *Evening Standard* had published ninety-eight articles by Socialists since they came to power; that there is no pressure from advertisers because half the amount of advertising offered must be rejected for lack of space; and that the public can restrain a newspaper by refraining from buying it.

Nonetheless the bill authorizing the Royal Commission was passed in 1946; seventeen members headed by Oxford Provost Sir David Ross were appointed in 1947; and in June 1949, the Commission delivered a 363-page report to Parliament. United Kingdom newspapers, it said, were "inferior to none," and while further mergers might be cause for concern, "we do not think that the present degree of concentration of ownership of the national press calls for any action." At the same time, it accused almost all papers of at least occasional news slanting—and the "popular" press of frequent slanting—and cited many instances of inaccurate and biased coverage. It also proposed a "general council of the press," consisting of "at least twenty-five members representing proprietors, editors, and other journalists, and having lay mambers amounting to about 20 percent of the total, including the chairman."

The Council, it said, was to safeguard the freedom of the press, improve methods of recruitment and training, censure "undesirable types of journalistic conduct, and by all other possible means, to build up a code in accordance with the highest professional standards." Activities would include hearing "complaints which it may receive about the conduct of the press or of any persons toward the press" and dealing "with these complaints in whatever manner may seem to be practicable and appropriate."

Most papers hailed the Commission report as an exoneration. Both the *Times* and the *Daily Telegraph* felt that improvements could only come from within, while the *Manchester Guardian* cast doubts on the sincerity of the "representatives of newspaper organizations, among whom dog does not usually eat dog." No major paper supported the proposal for a Press Council.

Publishers, clearly hoping to avoid carrying out the Royal Commission's mandate, drafted and redrafted their own plans for a council until January 1951. Then they consumed nearly two more years in discussions with journalistic organizations. Only after a threatening move in the House of Commons did they establish a council, but without lay membership. Lord Astor of Hever, chief proprietor of the *Times*, was appointed Council chairman (later to be succeeded by Sir Linton Andrews, editor of the Yorkshire *Post*, and then George Murray, a director of Associated Newspapers, Ltd.). Press organizations, however, provided so little money, and some large newspapers remained so aloof that the Council was hamstrung from the start. H. Phillip Levy, principal legal director to the *Daily Mirror* newspapers and chronicler of the Council, writes in his book *The Press Council*:

> While the maintenance of professional standards and integrity was an aim which all could support, there was a general feeling that an attempt to achieve this end through a disciplinary body would inevitably result in repressive measures restrictive of the freedom of the press. . . . The public, too, continued to regard the Council as a buffer against well-founded charges of newspaper misconduct.

A 1962 report by another Royal Commission, this one headed by Lord Shawcross, provided the impetus to reshape the Council into its present form. Since the first Commission report, ninety-eight newspapers and magazines had closed; control of approximately 75 percent of the national dailies' total circulation had fallen to three groups; and two groups had control of virtually the entire weekly periodical circulation. Only three cities in Britain outside London had fully competing local daily newspapers: Leeds, Glasgow, and Edinburgh. There also had been a series of spy scandals and charges of sensationalism surrounding coverage of such events as the romance between Princess Margaret and Group-Captain Peter Townsend; an air crash whose victims had been photographed; and the plight of Mrs. Donald MacLean after her husband's defection to Soviet Russia. If the press was not willing to establish a press council with the authority, financing, and public representation called for in 1949, said the Shawcross Report, then the case for a statutory body would be clear.

Thus goaded, journalistic organizations revised the Press Council's constitution. The new constitution was formally adopted on July 1, 1963, and the new General Council of the Press was convened on January 14, 1964, with twenty members representing the press and with Lord Patrick Devlin its chairman and one of five members drawn from the public at large. The Council's stated objectives read:

1. To preserve the established freedom of the British press.
2. To maintain the character of the British press in accordance with the highest professional and commercial standards.
3. To consider complaints about the conduct of the press or the conduct of persons and organizations towards the press; to deal with these complaints in whatever manner might seem practical and appropriate and record resultant action.
4. To keep under review developments likely to restrict the supply of information of public interest and importance.
5. To report publicly on developments that may tend towards greater concentration or monopoly in the press (including changes in ownership, control, and growth of press undertakings) and to publish statistical information relating to them.
6. To make representations on appropriate occasions to the government, organs of the United Nations, and to press organizations abroad.

7. To publish periodical reports recording the Council's work and to review from time to time developments in the press and the factors affecting them.

The Royal Commission had recommended that the chairman and lay members be nominated jointly by the Lord Chief Justice of England and the Lord President of the Court of Session of Scotland; in practice, press representatives on the Council make the nominations. The twenty seats allocated to the press are divided among eight organizations: the Newspaper Proprietors' Association, Ltd.; the Newspaper Society; the Periodical Proprietors' Association, Ltd.; the Scottish Daily Newspaper Society; the Scottish Newspaper Proprietors' Association; the National Union of Journalists; the Institute of Journalists; and the Guild of British Newspaper Editors.

All members are elected for three years and are eligible for reelection; professional organizations hold an unchanging number of seats and select their own representatives. Lay members have included a woman trade union official, a woman farmer, a woman barrister, a town clerk, a physicist, a schoolteacher, a clergyman, a brewery manager, and an engineer. Full council meetings, all of which are closed, are held at least five times a year; committee meetings more often. A staff of three professional journalists, headed by Noel S. Paul, Secretary, serves the Council full time. Annual operating expenses, now some $70,000, are funded by the professional journalistic organizations, with publishers bearing the largest share. A General Purposes Committee handles the "positive" aspect of the Council's work: actions on matters such as censorship, libel law, and compiling statistics on ownership concentration or monopoly in the press. The Complaints Committee considers grievances against the press.

No complaint is accepted until redress has been sought from the editor of the publication involved; then the grounds for complaint must be in writing, including copies of correspondence with the editor, a copy of the item complained about, and names and addresses of any persons who can provide additional information. If legal proceedings appear likely, complainants must sign a waiver of the right to use information developed by the Council in any legal proceedings, or must defer the complaint until court proceedings have been disposed of. About 20 percent of all complaints are eliminated in preliminary screening as frivolous or disclosing no case to answer. Of "effective" cases—those which go to the Complaints Committee or the full Council for action—at least half are rejected. Adverse adjudications of the Council are expected to be printed in the publications involved—and over the years all but five of more than a thousand adverse judgments have been published. This is the Council's only sanction. As Levy points out:

> The role of the Press Council is that of educator not inquisitor; its method is persuasion not force; its weapon is publicity not punishment; its appeal is to conscience and fair play. In a free press sanctions would be an incongruity.

One of the most publicized cases adjudicated by the Council involved the memoirs of former call girl Christine Keeler, a principal in the Profumo political scandal, as published by the Sunday *News of the World*. Miss Keeler's "confessions" already had been printed in the paper several years earlier; and in 1966, at the suggestion of the Council, British publications had drafted a declaration of principle barring payments for articles to persons engaged in crime or other "notorious" misbehavior "where the public interest does not warrant it." Even before publication—after promotion of the second Keeler "confessions" had begun—the Press Council condemned them as "an exploitation of sex and vice for commercial purpose," clearly in violation of the 1966 journalistic declaration of principle. The editor of the paper defended publication, holding that "while it is conceded that an influential minority argues against publication, the overwhelming weight of real public interest endorses publication." Despite his defense, however, the paper toned down the original copy somewhat.

Other typical cases:

— Condemnation of a *Daily Sketch* reporter after investigation showed that he had fabricated an interview with the director of a football team.

— Criticism of a reporter for a fictitious story of the capture of a fugitive, with the qualification: "The inaccuracy was due to the reporter being misled by false information supplied to him by a person who appeared, at the time, to be reliable. The Press Council accepts that the reporter and the newspaper acted in good faith and without negligence."

— Criticism of a paper for publishing a photo of a dead girl dangling from an aircraft.

— Declining to condemn two papers for publishing articles by wives of participants in England's Great Train Robbery, on grounds that the articles showed the criminals' insecurity and unease after the crime, thus emphasizing that crime does not pay.

The grievance procedure also allows citizen or press complaints about actions considered to impinge on press freedom. In
dealing with these, the Council frequently has directly fostered the
freedom to gather and disseminate news. In one case, it condemned a Parliamentary Conference proposal to forbid the publication of opinion surveys about elections for the seventy-two-hour
period immediately before the polls close. In another, after the
1966 disaster in which a landslide crushed part of a mining village
in Wales, the Council opposed an Attorney General's threat of
legal action against newsmen who interviewed witnesses; it issued a
booklet about government restrictions, urging that guidelines be
clarified for coverage of future disasters. A committee of inquiry
subsequently reported in the Press Council's favor. The Council
also has criticized local governmental bodies for excluding press
representatives, actively sought reform of libel law, and cam-
paigned for clarification of the legal status of "confidential information."

"The Council," said Lord Devlin, "will not accept that when
a document contains material of public interest the author can, by
rubber stamping it, impose an obligation of confidence on everyone into whose hands it may fall."

Levy credits the Council for the improved relations between
the media and the British public, and also for the greater amount
of space in the popular press now allotted to news (and a more
mature treatment of it).

Press Council Secretary, Noel S. Paul, whose judgment, tact,
and expertise have contributed greatly to the Council's acceptance, believes that progress has occurred in five areas: fewer
complaints about newsmen intruding into private lives of people in
the news; more corrections freely published by newspapers; clearer
boundaries between presentations of fact and opinion; fairer procedures for selecting and editing letters to the editor; and saving of
time and money of both newspapers and individuals by averting
many court actions. "I think it is certain that the reputation of the
press has been very greatly enhanced," he says, "not only by the
fact of the existence of a press council, but even more by the
acceptance, on a very wide basis, of the Council's role by editors
throughout the country."

"The Press Council," adds *Christian Science Monitor* reporter
John Allan May, "has been called a 'toothless bulldog'—as once
was Great Britain itself. But the requirements of a watchdog are
not that it should bite but that it should bark."

Significantly, when former United Press International London Bureau Manager Paul B. Snider surveyed attitudes toward the
Press Council, he found striking changes of opinion from the

initial antipathy shown. Ninety-one of one hundred and twenty editors responded, and seventy-nine questionnaires were tabulated. They showed that more than two-thirds of the responding editors professed to welcome the Press Council, while no respondents reported great resentment toward it.

William Rees-Mogg, editor of the *Times*, told the *Monitor*'s John Allan May: "[The Council] is doing very good work. There is no doubt it has markedly helped to raise the standard of journalism in Britain. I have not personally agreed with all its decisions, but they are taken seriously in Fleet Street. . . . I think the Council has also helped to take much of the sting out of the hostility that has existed towards the press here."

Simultaneously, however, hostility toward radio and television has grown, with the result that a counterpart council has been urged for those media. The BBC, after particularly harsh criticism of a 1971 program titled *Yesterday's Men*, agreed to set up an independent three-member Complaints Commission; the ITA agreed to create a small committee to handle complaints. Neither is strictly comparable to the Press Council. The BBC Commission (Sir Henry Fisher, former High Court Judge; Lord Maybray-King, former Speaker of the House of Commons; and Sir Edmund Compton, former Parliamentary Ombudsman) handles complaints from people or organizations who believe they have been unfairly treated in BBC programs; all verdicts are publicized in one of the BBC journals or, at the mandate of the Commission, on the BBC. Commission members serve three-year terms, with pay; have staff and offices independent of the BBC; and determine their own procedures, including how successors shall be chosen. The ITA committee is entirely an internal activity.

These new agencies, though, have not stilled agitation in Great Britain for a grievance body for broadcasting comparable to the Press Council. Nor, in the opinion of many observers, are they likely to do so. The media council idea seems too deeply rooted in British society for that to happen.

Press Councils in America

The first nationally publicized proposal to establish a press council in America came from the Commission on Freedom of the Press in 1947. Funded in 1943 by publisher Henry R. Luce and the *Encyclopaedia Britannica*, the Commission was chaired by Robert M. Hutchins, president of the University of Chicago. Members—none were journalists—included Zechariah Chafee of Harvard, Harold Lasswell of Yale, poet and former Assistant Secretary of State Archibald MacLeish, theologian Reinhold Niebuhr, economist Beardsley Ruml, and historian Arthur Schlesinger, Sr. Among its numerous recommendations was the "establishment of a new and independent agency to appraise and report annually upon the performance of the press." The body was to be "independent of government and the press . . . be created by gifts . . . [and] be given a ten-year trial, at the end of which an audit of its achievement could determine anew the institutional form best adapted to its purposes."

Former Senator William Benton of Connecticut proposed a similar body for radio and television in 1951, but recommended its creation by an act of Congress, with commission members to be appointed by the President. Other proposals followed.

— In 1961, John Lofton of Stanford's Institute for Communication Research suggested an institute to monitor and report on press performance.

— In 1963, University of Minnesota Journalism Professor J. Edward Gerald asked that a national council be formed and supported by journalism's professional and educational associations.

— In 1967, journalist and media critic Ben H. Bagdikian recommended that individual universities serve as press councils for their respective states.

— A 1968 meeting, convened by the National Institute of Public Affairs in Washington, outlined a plan for a national council of distinguished laymen to oversee monitoring of both broadcasting and print media.

— In 1970, a Task Force of the National Commission on the Causes and Prevention of Violence called for a national media study center "with a financing mechanism independent of the political processes; and with clearly delineated powers of monitorship, evaluation, and publication, but without sanction."

National press councils or grievance committees also have been proposed by the American Society of Newspaper Editors, the Association for Education in Journalism, and the National Conference of Editorial Writers. None of these proposals has been accepted.

According to Professor William L. Rivers of Stanford University, co-editor with William B. Blankenburg of *Backtalk: Press Councils in America* (San Francisco: Canfield Press, 1972), press councils at the local level were first suggested in the 1930s by Chilton R. Bush, head of the Department of Communication at Stanford. Though Bush promoted the idea among California publishers, there was little response until after World War II. In 1946, Raymond L. Spangler, editor of the Redwood City, California, *Tribune*, set up an advisory council of community leaders which met for about three months, and in 1950, William Townes, publisher of the Santa Rosa *Press-Democrat*, established a Citizens' Advisory Council to represent community interests such as labor, education, agriculture, city government, and business. This group lasted until Townes left the paper.

In 1951, *Editor and Publisher* said of the Council:

> On the practical side this particular newspaper reports that council meetings revealed several important stories that had not been covered. And council members felt free to visit the newspaper offices thereafter, something many of them might not have thought about previously. This is an experiment in getting closer to the community which strikes us as valuable. The good points

outweigh the bad, and if conducted properly and regularly can only result to the benefit of the paper.

The idea of local press councils again received national publicity in 1963 when Barry Bingham, Sr., publisher of the Louisville *Courier-Journal* and *Times*, proposed to the national convention of Sigma Delta Chi that local press councils be created. But no action resulted, even in Louisville.

It was not until 1967 that the local council idea received systematic trial. The Mellett Fund for a Free and Responsible Press, named for former Washington *Daily News* editor Lowell Mellett and administered by the Newspaper Guild, decided that the $40,000 in proceeds from a Mellett stock bequest to the Guild could most productively be used in local press council experiments. The president of the Mellett Fund, Ben Bagdikian wrote in *Backtalk: Press Councils in America:*

> The local press council appealed to the Fund for a number of reasons. First, it seemed eminently suited to American papers, which are local; whereas a national council would have to look at 1750 papers or a large sample of them. Second, it had never before been tried as independent projects carefully designed and recorded to produce a body of experience available to the whole trade. Third, a small number of projects could have a multiplied effect if results caused other publishers and other committees to make spontaneous efforts of their own. And fourth, we hoped we could afford it.

The ground rules were:

1. The local council would have no power, and no impression of power, to force change in the local paper. It could study, discuss, or vote, always with the publisher as a member of the group. But the paper retained discretion over its own contents.
2. The local council would not be organized by the paper. The Fund required that any proposal have the cooperation of the paper involved but the researcher would select council members, and members would understand that while they had no power over editing the paper, they were gathered as equals with the publisher in council proceedings.
3. The design implementation, and reporting of the council experience would be in the hands of a university researcher. Once the Fund was satisfied that the researcher was qualified and his plan met basic requirements, the Fund exercised no control over the experiment or over the researcher's report at the end of the year.
4. A major objective of the enterprise was to be a detailed analysis of the experience of the researcher, the results to be given the widest possible dissemination.

Under Mellett Fund auspices, press councils were established in Bend, Oregon; Redwood City, California; and Sparta and Cairo,

Illinois. In addition, race relations advisory councils were set up in Seattle and St. Louis. *Backtalk: Press Councils in America* is the official—albeit somewhat sketchy—report on all of the local experiments except for Seattle. That project is discussed in a 1969 report, "Seattle Communication Council of Media Leaders and Black Citizens," by Lawrence Schneider, who presided over the experiment while an assistant professor of journalism at the University of Washington.

William Rivers and William Blankenburg selected the members for the Bend and Redwood City councils. They also acted as staff directors and worked out procedures in consultation with the members.

The Mellett Fund councils had mixed results. Robert W. Chandler, editor of the Bend, Oregon, *Bulletin*, hailed the Bend council: ". . . it has created a defense mechanism for the press. It has been a power for good from my standpoint."

Indeed, in a six page facsimile fact sheet which he sends to persons who inquire about the press council there, Chandler says: "I am a missionary on the subject; I think press councils (or better yet, media councils including radio, TV, and local magazine, if they exist) are good things for the community and the cooperating media."[2]

Redwood City *Tribune* editor Spangler, now retired, says, "It was a very friendly experience for us. You know, editors tend to panic when they get three letters on the same subject. I think it served a purpose."

The Redwood council, however, was discontinued when Mellett financing, and the assistance of Rivers and Blankenburg, ended. According to David N. Schutz, editor of the *Tribune*, there are no plans to revive it.

"The Council here stopped operating primarily because the . . . experiment was for one year," he says. "However, we would not have recommended its continuance had the matter come to a vote. My basis for this reaction is that we seem to have accomplished little with the Council."

In the downstate Illinois town of Sparta, a Mellett Fund press council was initiated by journalism professor Kenneth Starck of Southern Illinois University, with the active cooperation of editor and publisher William Howe Morgan. Morgan was enthusiastic about the council experience and concurred with members' wishes to establish the council on a permanent basis. After the Mellett Fund experiment, the Sparta council reorganized, expanding membership to include high-school students, setting membership terms of three years, and scheduling quarterly meetings.

Press council advocate Norman E. Isaacs has referred to the Cairo, Illinois, experiment as "the only outright failure" among the Mellett Fund councils. Starck, in his report in *Backtalk*, acknowledges its difficulties, citing the racial clashes, but rejects Isaacs' characterization of the council as a "failure."

In a letter to the *Columbia Journalism Review* (Winter 1970-1971), he wrote:

> The Council did bring together blacks and whites . . . who remained active throughout its life. Two militant blacks were excluded from council membership—a stipulation by every person who was interviewed concerning council membership, including blacks who agreed to serve. This obviously was a flaw in council composition.
>
> Second, the council, despite frequent and heated discussion, survived the year-long experimental period and decided in favor of a permanent organization. Open warfare in the streets of Cairo negated that decision.
>
> Third, several positive changes did take place, presumably as a result of council sessions. A content analysis of issues of the Cairo *Evening Citizen*, conducted without the knowledge of officials of the newspaper, disclosed that it did not respond to some requests. . . .

The Cairo group probably should not be classified as a press council. It was created to deal with conditions that seemed similar to those that the Mellett Fund race relations advisory councils adressed in Seattle and St. Louis. The Seattle experiment, involving both print and broadcast media, was stimulated by Lawrence Schneider of the University of Washington; the St. Louis group by Earl Reeves, professor of political science at the University of Missouri.

In both cities, there were series of regular informal meetings involving media editorial executives and members of the minority-group community. The main purpose was to exchange ideas and allow minority-group representatives to describe their problems and grievances against the media—to open up channels of communication. Media members of the Seattle group unanimously endorsed the idea and expressed regret that meetings had terminated. After the Mellett grant expired, the group operated for a year on its own. But Schneider was unable to continue, and no other moderator was found. In St. Louis, where separate meetings were held with representatives of each media organization, media evaluations were unenthusiastic, but Professor Reeves concluded that the result had, on the whole, been constructive.

Elsewhere, similar race-relations advisory activities have been tried; among them the Boston Community Media Committee. This project was initiated in 1966 by basketball star Bill Russell, Boston *Globe* editor Thomas Winship, and other Bostonians. The Boston Community Media Committee has continued, expanding into such activities as recruitment and training of nonwhites for media employment, and creation of journalism curricula at high schools in predominantly black neighborhoods.

The Mellett Fund's example has stimulated establishment of several other press councils. One, in Littleton, Colorado, serves two weeklies: the Littleton *Independent* and the Arapahoe *Herald*. In 1946, Houstoun Waring, former principal owner and now editor emeritus of the papers, originated the Colorado Editorial Advisory Board to bring together newsmen from several Colorado papers and specialists in economics, political science, foreign affairs, and other subjects. He also established an Annual Critics' Dinner at which ten leading citizens described how they would run the Littleton publications. Upon learning of the Mellett Fund experiment, Waring and Garrett Ray, now editor and principal owner of the papers, decided to establish a council. Ray and Waring attend all council meetings and, through columns and editorials, apprise their readers of suggestions and criticisms by the council.

In February 1971, another council, established by the Hawaii *Tribune-Herald*, began operations in Hilo on the island of Hawaii. Named the Hawaii *Tribune-Herald* Press Advisory Council, it was initiated by the newspaper's newly promoted general manager, Leo Weilmann, formerly of the Pomona, California, *Progress Bulletin*.

Executives of at least two state newspaper associations also have suggested consideration of new councils in their states: John H. Murphy, executive vice president of the Texas Daily Newspaper Association, proposed some form of council in a 1970 memo to TNDA members; and the North Dakota Newspaper Association, at its 1972 annual meeting, formed a committee to study establishment of a council in the state.

In Canada, three provinces now have councils: Ontario, Quebec, and Alberta. The most ambitious effort, in Ontario, was organized under leadership of Beland Honderich, publisher of the Toronto *Star*. Chairman is A. Davidson Dunton, former editor of the Montreal *Standard*, former chairman of the Canadian Broadcasting Corporation (CBC), and former president of Carleton University in Ottawa.

Two of the most ambitious U.S. press council efforts—in Minnesota and Honolulu—are discussed in ensuing chapters.

Minnesota's Press Council

The most ambitious U.S. press council experiment is being carried out in Minnesota. There, at the initiative of the Minnesota Newspaper Association (MNA), a statewide council has been established to deal with grievances against newspapers anywhere in the state. Of its eighteen members, nine are representatives of the press and nine are public members. All eighteen were selected initially by the Minnesota Newspaper Association. Associate Justice C. Donald Peterson of the Minnesota Supreme Court is chairman.

The prime instigator of the Council, Robert M. Shaw of the Minnesota Newspaper Association, believes the locale of this most enterprising U.S. press council experiment is no accident. "I have the idea that Minnesota and our neighboring state of Wisconsin are two experimental states," he says. "They innovate in politics. ... A lot of good things in the way of new ideas, new experiments come out of Minnesota." Another factor is the nature of the Minnesota Newspaper Assocation. Unlike counterparts in many states, daily and weekly newspapers in Minnesota belong to one association, providing combined strength not only for lobbying, but for experiments such as the Press Council. The Association has a relatively young board of directors. In Shaw, it possesses a particularly vigorous, skilled, and courageous manager who regards his role as creative rather than ministerial.

Shaw studied philosophy at the University of Minnesota, but

took his Master's Degree in journalism. He studied briefly at the University of Heidelberg, worked for *Stars and Stripes* while in Europe, then on his return worked for the Associated Press. He managed a weekly newspaper in the state of Washington, taught for four years at the University of Washington School of Communications, and spent three years as chief executive of the Washington Newspaper Publishers' Association before returning to Minneapolis. He also has been president of the Newspaper Association Managers, Inc., the nationwide professional association for heads of associations of newspapers.

While in Washington, Shaw saw the Chief Justice of the State Supreme Court take the initiative in setting up a Fair Trial/Free Press committee shortly after the Samuel Sheppard murder trial in 1954. He regarded the idea as so worthwhile that upon arrival in Minnesota he persuaded the Newspaper Association to help set up a similar council. After a meeting with William Sumner of the St. Paul *Pioneer-Press* and *Dispatch*, he and Sumner met with Associate Justice Walter Rogosheske, who "caught the spark" and helped form the Fair Trial/Free Press Council, Inc. Justice Rogosheske has been chairman and Shaw secretary from the beginning. Shaw says:

> A committee of our Minnesota Newspaper Association had come out with what we called guidelines for the coverage of crime and the courts. That was the first step, really. On the basis of that we broadened our efforts and got other interest groups interested in a coalition. That gave us the training and the experience that made it possible for us to visualize what a press council could do. . . .
>
> In the Council, the first major thing we did was take the guidelines the Association had prepared and change them a little. This went on for a year. We had some heavy meetings and the thing almost collapsed a couple of times. The lesson to extract from that is that the kind of people you get on these things is basic. You've got to have people who are cool and don't feel that they have to take a position and then report to their constituency—who really have the authority to compromise. . . .
>
> So we redid our guidelines slightly and put them out with the blessing of the whole organization. These went to police and county attorneys and then to judges all over the state, and all of a sudden we got a lot of really good mail on it, saying it's a good thing. Most of the people I heard from . . . were not members of the press. I didn't have very many newspapers write and say 'Good work.' But I started to see that the judges and the lawyers and the like were looking at the press through different-colored glasses for the first time. You know, George Bernard Shaw says every profession is a conspiracy against the public. This easily can come true. But I could sense that this Fair Trial/Free Press activity was a good thing for us to do because it was the right thing to do.[3]

The idea of a press council germinated in the MNA's Goals and Ethics Committee in the spring of 1970. Gordon Spielman, a former New York labor organizer who moved to Minnesota to become publisher of a paper in the small town of Trimount, was chairman of the committee as well as an elected MNA board member. Another committee member was Philip S. Duff, Jr., publisher of the Red Wing *Republican Eagle*. Shaw says:

> One day the three of us were talking about how we ought to do more about ethics, because I would get all these squawks about newspapers and I didn't know what to do about them except to call the publisher and listen to him tell me to go jump. We don't really have any code of ethics except something we put up on the wall and then forget about—we don't have any working ethical instrumentality. So we decided that we should do more than we were, and to start by deciding what this committee should be. Then the question came up, should we add public members to our own committee? We thought maybe it would be a good thing because no profession can judge itself. We kept talking and we talked to other board members in that vein.

On September 18, 1970, the MNA Board of Directors, after several lengthy discussions, issued a procedure for hearing complaints before the MNA Goals and Ethics Committee. It stated in part:

> It should be emphasized to everyone that MNA has no binding authority to control actions of its members and seeks none. Instead, resting on the experience gained through the Fair Trial/Free Press Council of Minnesota, the association puts great confidence in the value of discussion as a way to resolve differences. It is conceivable that flagrant violation of ethics might require expulsion from MNA membership. However, this would be a matter for the Goals and Ethics Committee to recommend but for the MNA Board to decide. . . .

Procedures were then outlined for receiving written complaints and contacting the editor and publisher involved. It was specified that if the publisher and the complainant could not settle a grievance directly, the Committee was to arrange a meeting at "a location associated neither with newspapers nor with the business or profession of the complainant." It was noted that "there shall be no 'single finding' and both sides should be made specifically aware that the association is merely providing a forum to hear and to attempt to settle complaints."

On October 15, 1970, Dean Elie Abel of the Graduate School of Journalism at Columbia University delivered a lecture at the University of Minnesota sponsored by the Twin Cities Local of the Newspaper Guild. His topic was "The Press at Bay, 1970." Discussing problems of journalistic ethics and competence, he said:

I would submit that the time for letting things slide is past; that we are in something like a crisis of confidence, affecting all media, whether print or broadcast; and in my judgment we cannot much longer postpone a united effort to examine the shortcomings of the press—most broadly defined—to deal with that crisis by the most rigorous self-scrutiny.

It is my sober—and sobering—opinion that if we do not make the effort to police our own ranks, to label and expose malpractice where we know it exists, to raise and then maintain ethical standards, to deal honestly with the most vulnerable elements in the community, then others, less qualified and less kindly disposed, will move in and do the job for us. . . .

First, the job must be done by journalists sitting in judgment on their peers, not by outsiders; second, when fault is to be found it must be specific, naming names, so the public at large may know what is happening. . . .

And I have a modest proposal to put before you tonight. It is that these Twin Cities, Minneapolis and St. Paul, might show the way for the rest of us by setting up a Twin Cities Press Council right here. . . . The press council idea has not, till now, had a trial run in any metropolitan area of the United States. The Twin Cities strike me as perhaps the best place to determine whether it is an idea of value for the rest of the country. . . .

Abel's speech, reported in the Minneapolis and St. Paul papers, was noted and clipped by, among others, Shaw and Bernie Shellum, Statehouse reporter for the Minneapolis *Tribune*. Shellum, an active local Guild member, had led efforts to direct the Guild's attention beyond such concerns as pay and physical working conditions to such matters as newsmen's professional prerogatives. Shellum says:

I kept a clipping of the story lying around in my den for about a week, and then called John Carmichael, who is executive secretary of the Newspaper Guild of the Twin Cities. I said, "Let's do something about this. Let's arrange a tactical program here and make it work for us." He said, "That's a good idea." So we found a couple of other members who were interested in it and took it to the next executive board and conceived a plan. The challenge had been issued, so we simply asked the management of the newspapers here for an answer. The replies were quite equivocal, some negative and some merely vague. But the thing got bruited about and I think some people in the Minnesota Newspaper Association began wondering whether we might try to beat them to it and if so what position that might place them in.

Shaw and his colleagues pressed for expansion of the previously announced Goals and Ethics Committee complaint procedure. In December 1970, the MNA board approved establishment of a press council, and on January 14, 1971, Shaw invited representatives of the MNA and several guests for lunch to discuss the subject. Among the MNA representatives was Bower Hawthorne, editor of the Minneapolis *Tribune*, who, to the surprise of a number of MNA members, not only had been designated by the Cowles newspapers—the Minneapolis *Star* and the Minneapolis *Tribune*—to represent the firm in the deliberations, but had been designated with some enthusiasm.

"The *Star* and the *Tribune*," says Robert T. Smith, associate publisher of the Minneapolis *Star* and then its editor, "have had for a long time a strong feeling of responsibility to let the public have its say. We have probably published more letters-to-the-editor than any comparable newspaper. It runs about 1000 a month and sometimes we have had 30,000 letters a year. We and the *Tribune* have our 'ombudsman' activities called Reader's Referee and the Bureau of Accuracy and Fair Play. We seek out comments and complaints about our coverage. So we worried a little bit for fear something called an Ethics Committee or a Press Council would be set up and then develop into a sort of protective device; you would bring your complaints and that would be the end of it. . . . When it was clear that some of the editors of smaller papers whom we felt were responsible people were part of the effort we felt reassured. So when the MNA came to our publisher, Otto Silha, he could promise our support."

The January 14 luncheon produced a frank exchange. One guest contended that it was unwise for the Association to appear to control a press council by selecting its members and officially sponsoring it as an activity. Another said the MNA's suggestions were too much of a "package deal" and recommended a meeting of representatives of various groups to plan the council. Hawthorne moved that the MNA consult with Sigma Delta Chi, the professional journalistic society; other organizations such as the Minnesota AP Managing Editors' Association; the University of Minnesota journalism faculty; representatives of the working press; and others "which the Board considers might be interested with respect to recommendations for membership." Shaw was directed to prepare a memo that afternoon to MNA Board members so that the organization could "proceed with all deliberate speed to set up this council."

As Shaw readily concedes, it was of no small significance that, in addition to Abel's speech and previous activities of the Goals and Ethics Committee, several overt threats had been made to establish or try to establish press councils under state government auspices. Two years previously, he recalls, the Washington State Legislature had been presented with a bill to set up a government-sponsored press council appointed by the governor and funded by the state government. The bill was rejected. In July 1970, a convention of the Iowa American Legion had entertained a resolution to establish a government agency to deal with complaints against the media, then amended it to call on the press to establish its own "watchdog" agency to review complaints. And, as noted by Shaw in his January 14 memo to the MNA Board, a Minnesota State Representative announced that he was preparing legislation to set up a press council by statute. The council, if it found against the newspaper, would be empowered to prohibit the paper from receiving public legal advertising—a key source of revenue for many small papers—for one year. The council was to consist of a district judge and a representative of each of the two major political parties.

The MNA Board quickly approved the establishment of a press council, not merely on a local basis, but statewide, with equal representation for the public and the press. Shaw's steering committee then set about selecting its charter members. Shaw says:

> There was a lot of discussion about how do you choose public representatives, who represents whom, and so on, and we decided that we were not going to choose public members for their formal representation—that is, one person representing one group or one faction; we were just going to pick good public people for a balance between public members and members from the press. We decided that the group then would work out its own procedures, including its future relationship to the MNA, and the matter of its succession to membership.

Although a membership of fourteen originally had been informally agreed on, the Council as organized had a membership of eighteen. Associate Supreme Court Justice Peterson was named chairman. Other public members were: Dr. Malcolm Moos, president of the University of Minnesota and a former speech writer for President Dwight Eisenhower; Warren R. Spannaus, State Attorney General and former newspaperman; Mrs. Annette Whiting, of the state League of Women Voters; attorney and former State Senator Gordon Rosenmeier; Professors J. Edward Gerald (journalism) and Earl D. Craig, Jr., (Afro-American Studies) of the University of Minnesota; James L. Hetland, Jr., Minneapolis civic leader, law professor, and for six years executive director of the Metropolitan Council; and James Bormann, director of community relations for WCCO Radio (classified as a public member inasmuch as the Council was empowered to handle only matters concerning the print media).

Press members were Robert M. Shaw; Bower Hawthorne;

Gordon Spielman; Philip S. Duff, Jr.; Kenneth V. Hickman of the Grand Rapids *Herald-Review*; Lowell D. Mills of the Hutchinson *Leader*; Gerry Ringhofer of the Owatonna *People's Press*; Cecil E. Newman of the Minneapolis *Spokesman*; and Bernie Shellum, the only working reporter in the group, who was designated the Newspaper Guild's representative.

Announcement of the Council's makeup in February brought mixed reactions. Executive Secretary Carmichael of the Twin Cities Newspaper Guild wrote Justice Peterson that although the Guild believed the MNA "has performed a distinct service for the community in getting a press council 'off the ground,' the Guild felt the Council should become independent of the MNA." Carmichael also stated that the Council "does not give adequate representation to what we call 'the working newspaperman.'"

The Guild, however, decided to table competing proposals, partly on the advice of Shellum. "I am very favorably impressed by the quality of the people on the Press Council," he says. "The . . . Council has proved itself to be a malleable instrument. They have proved it by going along with some of the basic ideas that the Guild had espoused for a press council."

In March, Peterson appointed a committee to formulate a grievance procedure. In August, the committee submitted to the Council for approval a twelve-page document modeled on practices of the British Press Council (for complete text, see Appendix). On September 9, Justice Peterson called a news conference to announce that the proposed procedures had been approved by the Council and it was "now ready to receive complaints about the performance of newspapers in Minnesota." Complaints were to be sent to Professor Gerald, secretary of the Grievance Committee.

"If the Council finds the newspaper is not in error," the official announcement said, "it will attempt to resolve the misunderstanding by the complainant. If the newspaper is found to be in error, the findings will be transmitted to the newspaper, the complainant, and to the media for publication. . . . This is as far as the Council can go in imposing penalties for confirmed violations of good journalistic practices, but we believe such adverse publicity can effectively correct any abuses."

Some opposition to the Council already has surfaced within the MNA. While Shaw prefers not to elaborate, it is known that active opposition includes at least one upstate publisher still angry at the association for its opposition to the Newspaper Preservation Act. Although the Cowles papers in Minneapolis are participants, the Ridder papers in St. Paul are not. While Bernard Ridder, Jr., has been rumored to be actively opposed, persons who have spoken to him off the record report that he is not so much opposed as he is cautious, wanting to see how the Council develops before committing himself.

Financing remains a question. According to Gerald, based on his familiarity with the British Press Council, at least $10,000 a year are needed for a starting budget, but many services can be contributed by the University or other organizations. "We ought to be a going concern in the sense that the money comes out of Minnesota soil and serves Minnesota needs," he says, "but if we had money from outside we could use it to do research and to get organized." In the opinion of Gerald and others, radio and television also ought to be within Council purview, though admittedly this may not be imperative at the start. Also, of course, it remains to be seen how individual publishers will react—either in cooperating with the Council or in retribution against the MNA, which already has accepted a Council declaration of independence.

By early autumn 1972, the Council had delivered two formal "adjudications" without arousing evident opposition. One involved a labor newspaper's report that a Republican state legislative leader had dined with several lobbyists the night before legislative action favorable to the lobbyists. The legislator admitted eating at the restaurant named but provided evidence he had neither dined with nor conversed with the lobbyists. He declared his reputation had been damaged and requested a retraction. The publisher—a Council member—stood by the story, attributing it to confidential sources he declined to reveal, and disqualified himself from Council consideration of the case. The Council's decision, after reviewing the issues involved, defended the newspaper's right to confidentiality but held against the accuracy of its source and asked that the Council's decision be printed (which the paper did, followed a week later by comments in its own defense).

The second case involved a complaint that a small-town weekly, after publishing a letter anonymously, had privately identified its author to local officials. The Council held this to be improper on the grounds that the promise of anonymity in print implies complete anonymity.

Despite the admitted pitfalls, however, Shaw is optimistic. "It's kind of a gamble," he says. "But I don't think our Board would have done it if they hadn't sensed that we were strong enough to bring it off. The idea of cross-pollination of ideas is, I think, in the wind: the idea of at least one public member on professional licensing boards, etc. It ties in with the general frustration that people have about not being able to register their complaints, their feelings, in any effective way. This is no small item, the alienation of people, the lack of trust and faith in institutions."

John Cowles, Jr., president of the Minneapolis Star and Tribune Company, concurs:

> The Council has been formed mainly out of a general realization on the part of publishers of the credibility problem with the public. The potential gains seem likely to outweigh the potential risks. Sure, there are risks in terms of freedom of maneuverability, but there are gains in terms of credibility. The big gain can be in reinforcement of public confidence in the fairness of the press. It is awfully early to evaluate the Council. But locally we have no reason to regret it.

Honolulu's Community-Media Council

Honolulu is the largest American city to have attempted a press council. Its Honolulu Community-Media Council also is noteworthy for being larger than most press councils (thirty-one members), for encompassing both broadcasting and print news media, and for having been initiated by community sources rather than by a university representative or by a publisher or group of publishers.

The council's roots, it is generally agreed, lie in a lengthy dispute between Honolulu Mayor Frank F. Fasi and the Honolulu *Star-Bulletin*. Fasi, a veteran politician who has lost six elections and won three since 1950, has long been at odds with the press. During the 1968 election campaign, both the Honolulu *Advertiser* and the Honolulu *Star-Bulletin* editorially opposed the Mayor, but the *Star-Bulletin* was the more vehement. By the following spring, after still more *Star-Bulletin* criticism, the Mayor began to retaliate; he suggested, in speeches, that citizens would be far more likely to learn the truth from the Honolulu *Advertiser* than from the *Star-Bullein*.

In June 1968, *a Star-Bulletin* reporter attributed a plan for a skylift and restaurant on a local mountain landmark in part to an alleged strong supporter of the Mayor in the previous election. Fasi accused the reporter of deliberately attempting to discredit his administration and barred her from his office. The newspaper pointed out that the backer had not been mentioned in the story until the nineteenth paragraph and that the Mayor's rebuttal had been given a three-column headline. The Mayor requested that the reporter be removed from the City Hall beat. The *Star-Bulletin* demurred. The paper continued to print stories criticizing the Mayor, and in July, the Mayor took more severe action. He barred all *Star-Bulletin* reporters from his office and ordered department heads not to grant interviews to the paper.

The American Civil Liberties Union, Hawaii Newspaper Guild, AFL-CIO, the American Society of Newspaper Editors, and the Associated Press Managing Editors protested, but Fasi refused to lift the ban. That fall he even declined to talk to Associated Press reporters during a world tour after learning that AP stories were being filed about him at the request of the *Star-Bulletin*. On his return, he announced plans to sue the *Star-Bulletin* for $1 million.

As the impasse deepened a number of civic leaders expressed concern. One was the Reverend Claude F. Du Teil, rector of St. Christopher's Episcopal Church and an active crusader for social causes. In July 1969, he telephoned John Kernell, director of the City Office of Information and Complaints, to express his concern. "Something has to be done," said the clergyman. "Who is going to do it?"

After some discussion, Kernell said, "Well, on the Mainland they have experimented with press councils, and in England they have a really good one. I've got some material on it. Maybe something like that would help."

The Reverend Du Teil then called A. A. Smyser, editor of the *Star-Bulletin*, and George Chaplin, editor of the *Advertiser*. Both also mentioned a press council as a possible ingredient of a solution. The next call was to Dr. James A. Richstad, an assistant journalism professor at the University of Hawaii.

"I had," says Richstad, "coincidentally just returned from three weeks at the Stanford University Institute of Communication, directed by Dr. William L. Rivers, a key man in the Mainland community press council movement. We ended up with an organizing committee for a conference in January 1970. We wanted to see, number one, what relations were between the media and the citizenry. Was there a need for a press council? We didn't want to just organize something and find out there was no need for it."

Richstad, who had studied at the University of Washington and University of Minnesota and worked on newspapers in Seattle, Decatur, Illinois, and Honolulu, before joining the journalism faculty at Hawaii, knew the editors of both Honolulu papers well. Together they, the Reverend Du Teil, and others, planned a one-day conference for 150 persons at the University of Hawaii on January 13, 1970. Invited as special guest speakers were Douglass Cater, former Washington journalist and special assistant to President Johnson, and Robert W. Chandler, editor of the Bend, Oregon, *Bulletin* and participant in a pioneer local press council. Eight workshop panels were planned to discuss the relationship of the press to religion, the professions, labor-management, politics and government, community organizations, law enforcement, education and minorities, and poverty and protest. Gardiner B. Jones, associate editor of the *Advertiser*, reported on the following day that "the discussions . . . ranged far beyond the Fasi-*Bulletin* argument. Against the rising talk nationally of a media credibility gap, the conference revealed a deep public concern about the job being done by media and an equal concern by newsmen to have their function better understood. The upshot was a decision to explore what form and function of a community press council might best meet Honolulu's needs."

Harlan Cleveland, president of the University of Hawaii and a former staff member of *Reporter* magazine, was chosen to chair a steering committee to carry out the conference's mandate. On the day of the January conference, the *Advertiser* editorialized:

> The overriding point is that the news media—like everybody else these days—need better communication with the community they serve about the way they serve. We also feel there is a need for the community to better understand all the news media, for there is a vast body of ignorance and folklore about how news is gathered and presented. [A press council] won't solve anybody's credibility problem by itself but it does mean a worthy step in the direction of more mutual understanding.

Two days after the conference the *Star-Bulletin* editorialized:

> As seen by some conservatives, the press in Honolulu . . . is the handmaiden of the radical Left . . . but from the viewpoint of the leftist activists the press is a tool of the Establishment. . . . That these contrasting concepts of the media can and do coexist in one community (and they are only examples from a wide diversity) is reason enough to welcome the initiatives taken this week toward forming a community news media council. . . .
>
> The *Star-Bulletin* offers its fullest cooperation and other media also have indicated support. An effective council can look into community complaints about news coverage, try to understand both sides, and prod for improvement where it feels this is in order. It can in effect be the public's impartial intermediary or umpire. Its very existence seems likely to both spur the press to better performance and reassure the public about its media.

Cleveland's steering committee held a series of meetings and appointed thirty-one members to a larger planning committee. In

April 1970, it announced a unanimous vote to establish a permanent community-media council, and appointed a subcommittee consisting of Cleveland, the Reverend Du Teil, and Richstad to recommend council objectives and staffing and financing arrangements.

A week later Mayor Fasi quietly admitted a *Star-Bulletin* reporter to his office for a routine press conference. He still felt the newspaper's reporting was one-sided, the Mayor said, but the media council would "more or less ride herd" on the Honolulu news media by investigating complaints against them.

"I think everybody had been looking for a way out," says the Reverend Du Teil. "I think all of us were relieved that this had proved to be it."

On November 16, 1970, the steering committee presented to the thirty-one member temporary community-media council a set of guidelines recommending that "the starting membership of the council" should be the persons present. Hence this became the first gathering of the permanent Honolulu Community-Media Council.

The guidelines stated in part:

The primary purpose of the Council will be to serve as a community forum for discussions of policies and practices related to access to and public dissemination of information and how these affect the community, and to improve understanding between the mass media and the community.

A cardinal principle of the Council will be the preservation of freedom of the press.

The Council will concern itself in a positive way with the quality of information provided to the community by the mass media. . . .

The Council prefers that complaints in the first instance be made directly to the medium or media involved, and then to the Council if the news medium or media fail to give an answer satisfactory to the complainant. Complaints made by the news media may also be considered by the Council. The Council shall determine which complaints merit consideration.

The staff, under the direction of the Chairman, will prepare the agenda for each Council meeting, investigate complaints, research problems, prepare background materials, alert Council members to pertinent articles and other materials, and generally assist the Chairman and the Council to fulfill the objectives of the Council.

The Council shall operate to the extent possible by consensus, without elaborate rules of procedure. If necessary, it can act on motions by majority vote.

Meetings shall be held at the call of the Chairman, or on the request of any five members. . . .

The Council will encourage the development of codes of performance by the news media.

The regular Council meetings will be open. . . .

> The Council staff shall consist of a Director and University graduate students engaged to assist the Chairman and Director. Selection of individual students will be made by the Chairman and the Director.
>
> The Council will seek financing through application to local foundations, and the money will be channeled through the University of Hawaii Foundation, if agreeable to all parties. . . .

Gerald R. Corbett, retired Family Court Judge, was named Chairman. Corbett soon resigned for health reasons. Successor, business executive Nelson Prather, died in office. The Reverend Du Teil then served as Acting Chairman until October 1971, when Dr. Thomas Hamilton, former president of the University of Hawaii, was named Chairman. Members were drawn largely from established community institutions.

"We had discussed representation at the start," says Richstad, who is now a program director at the East-West Center in Honolulu, "and we decided that you are never going to get a really representative council no matter what you do, and there is no point in even pretending that you have 100 percent representation of the community. So what we wanted is people who got around a lot. They might be associated with one particular group, but also active in other groups. We didn't want a fellow standing up and saying, 'I speak for labor,' because he doesn't. Nobody can. But we do want a labor man there. So what we did was go through the list of people who attended the January conference and ask them if they were interested in continuing, and we invited thirty-one of those people."

Seven members of the Council, during the summer of 1971, were from the media: Chaplin, Smyser, Lark Daniel of the Hawaii Educational Television Network, Richard Daw of the Associated Press, Duane Harm of KHON-TV, Reid Hennion of United Press International, and John Kernell, who had left the city's employ for KGMB-TV-radio. And additional members came from church, educational, municipal government, military, community action, and other groups. These ranged from the Hawaii State Dental Association, Hawaii Employers Council, and the local Family Court to the United Public Workers Union, Youth Action, American Civil Liberties Union, and Susannah Wesley Community Center. Dr. Richstad is staff director.

"We set up a $16,000 budget," Richstad said last summer, "but so far we have run essentially on $150 left over from the January conference, plus several contributions up to $100 each from a community house, a labor organization, and individuals. Half of the budget was to be for research assistants—two scholarships or fellowships at the university for graduate students—one quarter of it for a part-time director, and the other quarter for office expenses. We also put in a small amount of money for an evaluation, in which at the end of a year we would send a questionnaire to our members and bring in someone who had worked with press councils on the Mainland to look over what we had done, make recommendations, and spend a few days with us writing a report. We had hoped to get aid from foundations, but thus far have been turned down. The result is that we are turning to council members to do research, and it seems to be working, although they still could use some support help. They're not going to go through the literature, but within limits they can do quite well."

Complaints about media action or other matters are directed first to Richstad, who ascertains that the media organization involved has been contacted and given a chance to work out any disagreement. The matter next is referred, in writing, to the Executive Committee or the Agenda Committee or both. If the preliminary decision is that the matter deserves further considera- tion, the Committee requests a reply to the complaint in writing. At that point the Agenda Committee recommends action—drop- ping the complaint, scheduling a hearing, or other disposition—and its recommendation is placed before the Media Council, whose meetings, approximately monthly, are open to the public.

"I expressed the feeling at the very first meeting," says Smyser, "that perhaps if we wanted to be an agency of reconcilia- tion rather than confrontation, closed meetings might be the best, because I felt that otherwise a handful of people might simply use the meetings as another forum for standing up and browbeating the press. But there was an immediate visceral reaction against the press having closed meetings, and I guess the point was a good one. As it happened, though the meetings have been announced in the press, the public attendance has been very limited—I don't think it has come to more than ten per meeting."

The Council's first meeting in November 1970—timed to coincide with the national convention of the Associated Press Managing Editors in Honolulu—was devoted largely to organiza- tional matters and to a panel discussion of coverage of the 1970 elections. The January 28 meeting dealt with a variety of substan- tive items:

— Concern was expressed about the sparseness of press listings of State Legislature committee meetings: only the name of the committee was listed without the subject of that day's hearings. Both papers' editors promised to check. Since then, the Legislature has provided more comprehensive information and the papers have printed it.

— The minister of a local evangelical church complained about lack of coverage of conservative religious groups and requested that newspapers print scriptural quotations and theological debates. In discussion, Council members suggested that other church groups might be more active in "making news"; that "hard news" and sermon material differed; and that extensive quotation of scriptures is not likely in news stories; and finally, that if the views of church groups about current issues were not being reported, a mechanical problem of newsgathering might be the cause.

— A council member questioned whether media coverage, especially by television, contributes to confrontations and disruptions. This prompted a lengthy discussion of media practices in covering demonstrations, riots, bomb scares, and other sensitive matters. Both editors and lay council members agreed that the issue was delicate, involving a fine line between the community's need for information and possible "multiplier" effects of coverage in sensitive situations.

In March, a memo was distributed to Council members summarizing bills in the Legislature that might affect the media. They included a bill requiring public officials to be available to newsmen for questioning "during office hours" and forbidding the barring of any reporter from news conferences; a bill to protect newsmen against being forced to disclose sources of information to any legal or legislative investigation; a bill requiring radio-television stations to keep and allow access to copies of scripts, videotapes, or tape recordings of editorials for five years; prohibition of cigarette and tobacco advertising in Hawaii; and a state version of the federal Newspaper Preservation Act.

The April 28 Council meeting dealt with still more varied concerns: a report of a meeting with news directors of the three Honolulu commercial television stations about procedures for covering demonstrations; the adequacy of the Council's membership policies and procedures; possible use of public television to spread information about the Council's activities; and a letter from a Council member on the use of terms such as "enemy" and "communist" in reporting from Indochina. A motion "to recommend that the local media utilize names used by organizations themselves that oppose us in Indochina rather than inventing or using other names" was voted down; a motion to form a committee to study the matter passed. Similarly, a discussion of sexism in advertising was referred to the Agenda Committee for recommendations.

One of the most vigorous discussions at the July meeting concerned the right of newspapers to lobby for such legislation as a local version of the Newspaper Preservation Act. Members considered whether the Council should take a stand on that question or the legislation itself. On the latter issue, one member said, "My feeling is that we should not, not just because of the tax-exemption factor, which may be important to us, but also because we then would become an instrument of the media or some other special group. The way I see this Council is as a place to clear the air, where the community and the media understand each other. Only in rare instances should we make motions. Airing the problem seems to be more important than an actual decision." And another member observed, "The point is that if we start getting involved in this kind of thing . . . we will destroy the Council—it will eventually get to be somebody's Media Council, somebody who has an axe to grind, whoever has the most muscle, pushing for certain kinds of legislation. . . . This is the one place I feel that we can have a discussion so that we understand each other better. And the position of some of the community organizations and even pressure groups, should simply be that they want the representatives of the media to know how they feel if they think they are being unfairly treated. And I think that does have an effect on what the media do."

The most publicized action of the Honolulu Council—its position concerning terminology in Indochina coverage—also was discussed. First, three responses to letters from the Council were read. In one, Arthur Ochs Sulzberger, publisher of *The New York Times*, wrote that he "deeply appreciated" the resolution of the Council and "the support it contained." A letter from H. L. Stevenson, then managing editor of UPI, expressed support for the Council's position and enclosed a copy of the *UPI Reporter* for July 15, which stated in part:

> Since the China debate was touched off in the June 10 *UPI Reporter* by a recommendation from Hobert E. Duncan of the Honolulu *Star-Bulletin*, it should be noted that the Honolulu Community-Media Council on June 21 adopted a resolution urging all national media to avoid certain terms and to substitute others in connection with the war in Vietnam.
>
> The resolution noted a decrease in recent months in use of the terms "Communist" or "red" in reference to China and said: "More accurate reporting has led to the use of such terms as 'Mainland' and/or 'People's Republic.' "

The Council expressed concern over the use of such umbrella terms as "Communist" or "enemy" to describe political or military groups or forces in Indochina. Its resolution went on to say:

These terms should be avoided as much as possible in favor of more descriptive terms which accurately designate the people or organizations to which they refer. In this regard we recommend the following questions as guidelines:

a. When opposing forces meet, who actually makes up the opposing forces? What organizations are involved? Does the word "Communist" accurately describe who they are? Can everyone who is fighting against the South Vietnamese government be described as a "Communist"?

b. When death tolls are announced, who actually has been killed? Are they military personnel, or are they civilians? Can everyone who is killed be accurately described as an "enemy"? Is a person an "enemy" simply because he has been killed by the South Vietnamese? (See Senator Kennedy's subcommittee report on refugees and civilian casualties.)

It is good to note that the resolution acknowledges the difficulty in sometimes ascertaining the precise identity of political or military groups in Vietnam. When a mortar shell hits a town or base, for example, there is often no way of knowing whether it was fired by North Vietnamese or Vietcong units. Hence the use of "Communist" to cover both possibilities.

It is our practice to avoid the use of "enemy" unless we are quoting some communique, declaration, or statement in which it is used. The news dispatches of an international news agency go to news media in many countries that are uninvolved in the Vietnam conflict and "enemy" would clearly be objectionable to them.

We certainly agree with the Honolulu Community-Media Council that specifics are preferable to generalities and should be used wherever possible.

The Honolulu Council still faces many difficult questions. One is financing. Another is defining the Council's mission and broadening its membership. One of the evaluations commissioned by the Council in 1972 was made by former *Time* correspondent Serrill Hillman; it stated that "What is really needed is a sense of importance and, as one member put it, a lively presentation of issues, so that neither council members nor public are bored."

Hillman suggested employment of paid staff members, involvement of "people who really care," replacement of "dead wood," and broadening of the membership base "with more activists, representatives of the student underground press, more women, more non-Caucasians, more people from outside Honolulu proper."

Lawrence S. Berger, principal owner and manager of KHVH radio and television (ABC Television, CBS Radio), resigned after the first Council meeting. In his view the Council is "a sort of glorified press club," with "a couple of do-gooders and a few media people who wanted to launch it."

But Richstad is hopeful. "I think the Council is settling into a structure," he says. "I think that what we are doing is basically right. I see a lot of need for improvement. I think we need more research, and if we don't get funding that is going to be a continuing problem if we are going to make our reports signifi-cant. I think the Council has enough strength at this point and enough support so that it will continue. In fact the urge among the Council members has been to become more active, to meet more regularly, to go into more detail on these issues, so I don't think they'll decide to disband. They seem to want to come to more resolutions than we have been coming to."

Editor Smyser of the *Star-Bulletin* says:

> In most cases I think the Media Council has more or less backed us up. I believe the Council will in time encourage us to change our ways. I hope it also will give some people a better understand-ing of our problems and what we are trying to do. . . . the fact that there is a court of appeals, if you will, independent of the press, I believe will take some of the sting out of the feeling that we have a monopoly press in the community which is high-handed and arbitrary and beyond reason. . . .
>
> I have a cautious optimism. I think there are pitfalls ahead and I think that very much depends on who comes along as a leader. If any leader takes over the group with the intent of turning it into a forum for simply abusing us I think we'll simply drop out. We don't need to cooperate in a self-flagellation exercise. . . .
>
> We would like to see the Council work—for our own good and for the community's good. The question of the credibility of the media is a fairly important one, not only to the media but to the community. If you don't have credible media your community is in trouble. So if this can help to reassure people that we aren't as bad as our worst critics think, though maybe not as good as we say we are, I think it might be all to the best.

What of the Future?

Reviewing the various experiments for making the news media more responsive to the public, it is plain that "something is happening out there"—that "consumerism" has caught up with the press and that changes are taking place in the media environment. Both professional journalists and significant segments of the public want a larger voice in setting standards for the communications media, and they intend to be heard.

There are no panačeas, either for the shortcomings of the press and broadcasting or for halting unfair or uninformed criticism. But there are steps that might be taken to help the press and broadcasting improve and foster public understanding of their problems. What agents for change seem promising? To what kinds of media checks and balances is the public entitled? And what are their limitations?

In the case of journalism reviews and city magazines, the most obvious limitation is one of coverage; they are, and always will be, too few, compared to the number of media organizations. The circulation of each is limited, even in its chosen area of concern; quality is uneven and may not reflect the views of broad segments of a community; and, perhaps most important, because of these organs' limited exposure, they are too easily ignored. Not that they have no influence; some influence is demonstrable. But at best they can do only part of what needs doing.

"Reporter power" efforts are similarly limited and, equally

important, depend for success in part on outside influences—publicity and peer-group checks on retribution against staff members who raise embarrassing questions. Moreover, only the relatively small number of newspapers with "elite" or semi-elite pretensions probably are susceptible to change through such editorial staff activity. Whereas newspapers such as *The New York Times, The Washington Post,* the *Wall Street Journal, The Los Angeles Times,* and a few others must attract and hold high-quality staff members in order to maintain self-chosen standards, in most newspapers reporters do not have enough leverage to affect policy significantly.

Citizen-group efforts have great potential for influence on broadcasting, which is publicly licensed and regulated. This potential, which can be used for good or ill, tends to alarm broadcasters to the point that some react to the smallest, softest noises. The more profit oriented the broadcaster, and therefore perhaps the more deserving of criticism for neglect of public service, the more this is true. To date, however, only fairly broad-based groups with specific, constructive goals—truth in advertising, opposition to "commercial clutter," counteracting blatant neglect of public service programming, or changing conspicuously questionable employment policies—have really been influential. The print media for the most part have been beyond reach of such citizen action, except concerning truth in advertising.

Newspaper "feedback" features and ombudsmen also have been constructive, but again coverage has been limited. In the case of ombudsmen, expense is another problem—a senior editorial staff member must be freed for almost full-time duty as ombudsman, a manpower allocation that budget-conscious publishers hesitate to make. Any such ombudsman arrangement, moreover, may be viewed with suspicion as a "house" operation.

What of press or media councils?

In Britain, the Press Council seems to have served a constructive purpose. Despite imperfections, it has become a forum, reasonably acceptable to public and press, in which grievances against the press can be aired. Only a few of its findings have not been publicized by the media adversely judged, and important actions receive enough publicity to have impact. Some of the most free-wheeling practices it has criticized are now less prevalent, and it has sufficient credibility to be an effective advocate for press freedom.

Critics are correct in accusing the Press Council of failing to transform the more sensational elements of the British press. They often ignore the point, however, that some sins have been curtailed; that if there were no Council the press might be worse; and that the Council does provide a recourse for citizens who previously could only take grievances to the courts or to elected officials. Moreover, the Council's existence has provided enough of a safety valve to help the press survive perhaps the most difficult period in modern British history with its freedom essentially intact. These are scarcely negligible accomplishments.

For various reasons, the British experience probably is not precisely transferable to the United States. Britain is, first of all, far smaller and more homogeneous than the United States, making the logistics of its press council simpler; it has several large national daily newspapers; the United States has two (*Wall Street Journal, Christian Science Monitor*); it has fewer newspapers than the United States; and its publishers were under greater pressure, directly from Parliament, to accept a press council than U.S. publishers ever have been. Nonetheless, some form of the press council seems workable in the United States.

Would editors accept a media council? Editors oppose, necessarily, any dictation of news judgments from outside their organizations. Media councils cannot dictate. Editors oppose, again necessarily, anything which significantly intrudes on their already overburdened schedules. Media councils tend to save, rather than waste, editorial staff time; when cranks or pressure groups keep returning, one can simply suggest, "Maybe you had better go and see the media council."

Editors oppose, justifiably, any organization which could lead to government regulation of the media. Media councils forestall, rather than foster, government regulation. Editors also oppose anything which might compromise confidentiality of news sources. Press councils defend confidentiality—and need not necessarily even inquire into the identity of confidential news sources in order to evaluate most aspects of sensitive news stories. Surely the frequency with which this issue has recurred in recent months serves to underline the urgency of the need for such defense. In any case, administrative discretion about when to press the point can avoid destructive and counterproductive confrontations.

Editors oppose, understandably, any program that is merely an institutionalized form of *mea culpa*. Media councils tend to protect their status and self-respect by requiring dignified proceedings. Editors, again understandably, do not wish to be party to publicizing black marks against them. Media councils invariably return a majority of decisions in favor of editors, and even adverse decisions tend to include enlightening explanations of why editorial decisions made in good faith were difficult. Above all, as several

U.S. editors who have participated in establishment of media councils have pointed out, whenever a media organization's self-interest ceases to be served by cooperation with a council, it can withdraw its cooperation.

If these points are valid, why have U.S. editors not established a national council or many more local or state councils?

The American Society of Newspaper Editors (ASNE), as previously noted, has debated setting up a national ethics or grievance committee to deal with specific complaints about coverage. Pressure from publishers on editors, however, as well as the genuine reservations of some editors about the suitability of ASNE for such a task, has kept the proposal from a floor vote. Some editors question ASNE's ability to finance a national activity such as this. They are reluctant to sit in judgment on colleagues, and wonder whether the public would look upon judgments by an editors' organization as a "whitewash." Further, they understandably fear opposition from publishers—who tend to be more conservative than editors and tend to wish to discourage dialogue about such questions as multiple-media ownership, advertiser influence, and the like. Several prominent editors are known to be so vehemently opposed to ASNE assumption of such a responsibility that action seems unlikely.

If one examines the record closely in Britain and the United States, it seems reasonable to question whether editors or publishers should be expected to initiate a press council. In Britain, the motivating force clearly came from the outside—public sentiment expressed directly through Parliament. In councils affiliated with the Mellett Fund, the initiative was provided by the Fund. In Minnesota and Honolulu, real or anticipated problems with public officials were factors. Similarly, although the press and bar have established Fair Trial/Free Press committees jointly, it was the bar that initiated them.

In any case, a *comprehensive* national press council covering *all* U.S. daily and weekly newspapers is probably not feasible at this time. Such a council would probably have to grow from the ground up—possible as a federation of local or regional councils— rather than appear full-blown at this early stage in U.S. experience with such organizations. John Cowles, Jr., president of the Minneapolis Star and Tribune Company, observes:

> It is one thing for people in journalism and the readers to keep track of newspapers in their hometown or in a whole state; it is another in a larger area. The problem is one of scale. If a national council comes, it may be in a scattered, heterogeneous way, through state and local councils which can work with and talk to each other.

But several other arrangements for monitoring the media on a national scale probably are feasible now. The American Society of Newspaper Editors, for instance, or the American Newspaper Publishers Association could establish and fund an independent ombudsman who, with a paid staff, could act on major complaints about the media. A multi-function national media institute, such as that proposed by former presidential assistant Douglass Cater, could be set up to fulfill some of these functions. As envisioned by Cater and an Aspen Institute workshop group, the new organization could, among other activities, sponsor reports and seminars on media problems, foster advanced-study fellowships, and maintain some limited form of ethics and grievance machinery. Public television could carry a national media review and critique. A limited-scale national media complaints council could monitor only the national media "wholesalers": the wire services, news magazines, radio-television networks, and "supplemental" spot-news wire services such as those of *The New York Times*, Chicago *Daily News*, and *The Washington Post-Los Angeles Times*.

If further experiments with councils are contemplated, several points should be kept in mind:

1. No media council can succeed without the cooperation of a majority or a "critical mass" of major media organizations within the council's jurisdiction. This need not mean participation of all the media in an area; once a council has established an operating norm, some previously reticent organizations can be expected to cooperate, or at least not to oppose it actively.
2. The necessary nucleus of organizations probably can be persuaded to participate if a council's auspices are so broad that it is in the media's interest not only to participate but also not to appear to obstruct. This means that any serious proposal for a media council probably must come from a group with a somewhat establishmentarian tinge; it does not mean that nonestablishment segments can or should be excluded from participating.
3. Careful thought should be given to selection of council members—especially the chairman. Though the council may have an establishmentarian tone, social "fringe" organizations should feel they have access to it, through direct representation or through sincere efforts by council members to be "honest brokers."
4. A council's geographical jurisdiction should be appropriate to the circumstances. Where a large urban area is

involved, there may be good reason for having more than a local press council; few organizations find it congenial to criticize or be criticized by a competitor located "right down the street." Special-purpose groups, for example, race relations councils, may be more promising for very large metropolitan areas or for smaller towns such as Cairo, Illinois, which are badly fragmented over the racial issue. If a state or regional council is contemplated, the participation of some large metropolitan papers can be crucial to attracting smaller newspapers, and without the larger papers, the council's credibility can be crippled. New England might be a promising base for a regional council, Texas, among other states, for a statewide council.

5. Journalism schools have important potential as initiators of councils; in any case, some academic input is useful both for assistance in organizing and for staff-secretarial activities. Every successful council has had an academic "resource" person on call or participating regularly.

6. A self-appointed public group, usually involving media representatives, normally is needed to select the original members of a council, which then can broaden its charter as desired. Despite the inherent disadvantages of this arrangement, there seems to be no pragmatic alternative. To an extent it is self-correcting; an unrepresentative council has so little chance of success that neither the media nor any organizing group would have much incentive to establish one. Once organized, the council can establish its own procedures and criteria for succession.

7. Although councils have generally excluded broadcasting from their purview on the grounds that it is a licensed industry, voluntary cooperation by broadcasters on specific kinds of complaints should be encouraged.

8. While modest funding from foundations or comparably disinterested sources can be helpful, lack of money should not be regarded as an obstacle to media council experiments. Money appears to be needed now most urgently for information dissemination to and among various councils or citizen groups interested in trying to establish councils.

A final *caveat*: just as it is shortsighted to reject out of hand serious proposals for such innovations as media councils, it is equally unwise to advertise councils as a cure-all. A council should be looked upon simply as a useful forum for discussion and consideration of correctives for the shortcomings of the news media, for an exchange of views about press and broadcasting problems, for a demonstration of good faith by media representatives who profess genuine interest in fulfilling their responsibilities as well as claiming their rights, and for experimenting with new liaison methods with a concerned public whose support is imperative if press freedoms are to be maintained.

The social upheavals which shook the sixties are far from over. Rapid change, with its disorienting and sometimes violent manifestations, will persist. The news media, as portrayers of that change and interpreters of its consequences, cannot escape the storm. If they do not recognize the forces at work to humanize institutions, expand consumer participation in the marketplace, and allow individuals in our mass society to preserve a personal franchise, then the consequences may be serious indeed.

Notes to Background Paper

1. These range from a right-wing organization with one professional staff member—Accuracy in Media (AIM) in Washington—to the more widely based Action for Children's Television (ACT) and the Office of Communication of the United Church of Christ, which has been prominent in reducing abuses of the Fairness Doctrine and in broadening employment and programming practices at several stations and station groups.

2. In describing the Bend council, Chandler comments, "Our original council included two of the community's most severe critics of our newspapers. I would suspect if it is to have any real benefit either to the newspaper or the community such persons should be included on others." Each member of the Council serves a three-year term, with three terms expiring at the end of each year. New members are chosen by vote of the Council, with the newspaper having no voice in their selection—although, says Chandler, "Council members have asked us for nominations and some of our nominees have been selected." The first year, under Mellett Fund financing, William Rivers attended each meeting and acted as moderator. He had no vote, only a mandate to prepare an agenda for each meeting, to preside, and to sum up discussion on each point and, when the Council wished, to make the

results of that discussion known to persons not at the meeting. Chandler feels that faculty members from neighboring journalism schools can play roles similar to that played by Rivers. The complaints of inaccuracy that were brought before the Bend council, according to Chandler, came from small stories picked up from the police blotter. "Police reporting is at fault in many cases; in other cases the argument is with the policeman over interpretation of facts (whose car collided with whom). Council members are not concerned with the views expressed in editorials unless those views are expressed in news stories which appear on other pages. They understand the editorial page is the place for me to express my own views and prejudices. But that doesn't mean questions aren't asked." As the Council developed, Chandler found it advisable that he, rather than reporters, attend meetings to act as middleman and to avoid personal confrontations. He said, however, that someone from the paper should attend every meeting.

3. Shaw says that when a member of the newspaper association called up with a problem a meeting would be held with the various parties concerned. "So another lesson that came out of this was that the mere fact that you had a mixed group means you've got what I call a coalition of interested people, including the state Supreme Court, who are concerned about this. They have no authority whatsoever—we have insisted all along that the only authority we have is the value of discussion itself. . . . One big surprise which changed my philosophy on this whole matter is that the greatest defenders of a free press are not generally the press. They come out of the woodwork . . . some fellow you thought was going to be an enemy comes out sounding like Supreme Court Justice Hugo Black. . . . Mix up the police and the lawyers and the judges and the newspapermen [in a meeting together]—everybody involved in any kind of social question—and that is the way we learn, because when we meet ourselves we keep saying the same kinds of things that we have heard over and over again, the things that make us feel good, not the things that do not."

Bibliography

Books

Commission on Freedom of the Press. *A Free and Responsible Press*. Chicago: University of Chicago Press, 1947.

Gerald, J. Edward. *The Social Responsibility of the Press*. Minneapolis: University of Minnesota Press, 1963.

Hohenberg, John. *Free Press/Free People: The Best Cause*. New York: Columbia University Press, 1971.

Levy, H. Phillip. *The Press Council: History, Procedure and Cases*. New York: St. Martin's Press, 1967.

Murray, George. *The Press and the Public: The Story of the British Press Council*. Carbondale, Ill.: Southern Illinois University Press, 1972.

Rivers, William L., and Schramm, Wilbur. *Responsibility in Mass Communications*, rev. ed. New York: Harper & Row, 1969.

Rivers, William L., Blankenburg, William B., Starck, Kenneth, Reeves, Earl. *Backtalk: Press Councils in America*. San Francisco: Canfield Press, 1972.

Special Canadian Senate Committee on the Mass Media. *The Uncertain Mirror*. Ottawa, Canada: Queen's Printer for Canada, 1971.

Periodicals

Altschull, J. Herbert. " 'Moment of Truth' for the BBC." *Columbia Journalism Review*, November/December 1971.

Balk, Alfred. "Minnesota Launches a Press Council." *Columbia Journalism Review*, November/December 1971.

Barron, Jerome. "Access to the Press—A New First Amendment Right." *Harvard Law Review*, 1967, pp. 1641-78.

Blankenburg, William B. "Local Press Councils: An Informal Accounting." *Columbia Journalism Review*, Spring 1969.

Chandler, Bob. "Editor's Bane or Salvation?" *Bulletin of the American Society of Newspaper Editors*, May 1969.

Evans, Harold M. "Is the Press Too Powerful?" *Columbia Journalism Review*, January/February 1972.

Huston, Luther. "Noyes Urges ASNE Members to Guard Their Perspective." *Editor and Publisher*, April 17, 1971.

Isaacs, Norman E. "Why We Lack a National Press Council." *Columbia Journalism Review*, Fall 1970.

Markel, Lester. "Why the Public Doesn't Trust the Press." *World Magazine*, August 15, 1972, pp. 36-39.

Paul, Noel S. "Why the British Press Council Works." *Columbia Journalism Review*, March/April 1972.

Schneider, Lawrence. "A Media-Black Council: Seattle's 19-Month Experiment." *Journalism Quarterly*, Autumn 1970.

Tobin, Richard L. "Does the U.S. Need a National Press Council?" *Saturday Review*, October 14, 1967.

Newspapers

Gereben, Janos. "Media Council Has Tired Blood." Honolulu *Star-Bulletin*, July 6, 1972.

King, Seth S. "Minnesota Forms a Press Council." *The New York Times*, January 28, 1972.

Lowman, Ron. "The Press Council Can Rap Publishers' Knuckles." Toronto *Star*, July 21, 1972.

Rigert, Joe. "Press Council and the Public." Minneapolis *Tribune*, February 6, 1972.

Smyser, A. A. "Sizing Up the Media Council." Honolulu *Star-Bulletin*, February 1, 1972.

Walz, Jay. "A Press Council Set Up in Ontario." *The New York Times*, August 20, 1972.

Wehrwein, Austin C. "The News Business: Can the Press Police Itself?" *The Washington Post*, March 14, 1972.

APPENDICES

Constitution of the
Minnesota Press Council

I. *Title*—The Minnesota Press Council, hereinafter called the Council, is a voluntary extra-legal body constituted on and from February 19, 1971.

II. *Purpose*—The purpose of the Council is: (A) to preserve the freedom of the press; (B) to maintain the character of the press in accordance with the highest professional standards; (C) to consider complaints about the conduct of the Minnesota press, including advertising, as well as the conduct of persons and organizations towards the Minnesota press, and to deal with these complaints in whatever manner is reasonably practical and appropriate; (D) to review, on a continuing basis, the performance of the Minnesota press regarding matters of general public interest; and (E) to urge and assist the Minnesota press in the fulfillment of its unique responsibility to perform in the public interest.

III. *Membership*—

A. The Council shall consist of eighteen members selected from the following groups:

1. Nine of the members shall be selected from the general Minnesota public at large.

2. Nine of the members shall be selected from members of the Minnesota press. At least two of these members shall be non-management and non-ownership members of the press.

B. New members on the Council shall be selected by members on the Council. Such members shall be selected in equal proportions to their representation on the Council as provided in paragraph B of this Article III.

The total membership on the Council may be increased to a maximum of twenty-four members. If additional members are added to the Council, they shall be selected in equal proportions to their representation on the Council as provided for in paragraph A of this Article III. A decision to increase the membership on the Council shall require the approval of the two-thirds majority of the members present and voting at a meeting, which two-thirds majority shall not be less than a simple majority of the membership of the Council. No decision to increase the membership on the Council shall be effective unless at least twenty-eight days' notice of such proposed action shall have been given in writing to all Council members.

C. Upon nomination to the Council, a person shall be entitled to membership for three consecutive years. At the end of this period the member, if he or she is qualified, shall be eligible for reappointment. Upon first appointment of the group of members specified in paragraph A of this Article III, six shall serve for only one year before retirement and a further six for an initial period of two years. These members shall be decided by lot. They will be eligible for reappointment, and thereafter the normal period of their membership on the Council and that of their successors shall be three years.

D. Any member of the Council ceasing to be qualified as a member of the Minnesota press or as a non-management or non-ownership member of the Minnesota press shall notify the Secretary of the Council within one calendar month of the change in his, or her, status, and his, or her, membership shall thereafter terminate within three calendar months. A person filling such a vacancy, or any vacancy on the Council, shall be appointed to membership in like manner to that by which the person whose vacancy he, or she, fills was appointed. Upon initial appointments he, or she, shall retain membership only for the expired portion of the period which remained to the person whose place on the Council he, or she, takes.

IV. *Officers*—At the first meeting of the calendar year, the Council shall elect from its membership a President, a Vice-

President, and a Treasurer, who shall serve terms of one year. The Council shall also elect a Secretary, who need not be a member of the Council, and who shall serve at the pleasure of the Council.

The President shall be the presiding officer at the meetings of the Council. He shall be the spokesman for the Council. He shall, with the approval of the Council, appoint committees and sub-committees to report to the Council. He shall cause to be distributed a summary of each meeting to the members of the Council.

The Vice-President shall preside at all meetings when the President is not in attendance and shall automatically assume the presidency whenever a President resigns or for any reason ceases to be an active member of the Council.

The Secretary shall perform the usual duties of a Secretary, including but not limited to, sending out notices of all meetings and recording and preserving the minutes of all meetings. The Secretary, at the direction of the President and the chairman of the Grievance Committee, shall also investigate such matters and complaints as the Council shall, from time to time, deem necessary.

The Treasurer shall be responsible for establishing a procedure for the collection of dues and contributions, and accounting for all receipts and disbursements at each annual meeting. The Treasurer shall be bonded in an amount approved by the Council. He may, with the consent of the Council, appoint a deputy who also shall be bonded in the same way.

Should a vacancy occur in the office of the Secretary or of the Treasurer, successors shall be elected by the Council.

V. *Quorum*—A quorum at the Council meeting shall be one-half of the voting members of the Council plus one member.

VI. *Committees*—The President shall, with the approval of the Council, appoint committees of its members for the discharge of such duties as the Council shall from time to time specify.

VII. *Procedures*—Each member of the Council shall be entitled to cast one vote in any matter decided by them on a show of hands or by ballot. All parties to a grievance shall have the opportunity to appear in person before an appropriate Council body considering the grievance to give evidence and present testimony.

The Council shall have no direct or coercive powers. Its actions shall be limited to the issuance of public statements expressing the Council's views.

VIII. *Finances*—Funds for the operations of the Council may be obtained by dues and contributions.

IX. *Amendments or Repealers*—Amendments to or repealers of any Articles of the Constitution shall require the approval of a two-thirds majority of the members present and voting at a meeting, which two-thirds majority shall not be less than a simple majority of the membership of the Council. No amendment or repealer shall be effective unless at least twenty-eight days' notice of a proposed amendment or repealer shall have been given in writing to all Council members.

X. *Dissolution*—The Council may at any time terminate its existence. A resolution to dissolve the Council, to be binding, must be passed by a two-thirds majority of its members present and voting at a meeting specially called for that purpose, which two-thirds majority shall be not less than a simple majority of the membership of the Council. Not less than twenty-eight days' notice shall be given of any such meeting and such notice shall give particulars of the purpose for which the meeting is called. Upon dissolution all remaining unencumbered funds shall be contributed to the University of Minnesota to be used for scholarships in its School of Journalism and Mass Communication.

Grievance Committee Procedural Rules, Minnesota Press Council (1971)

One of the primary functions of the Minnesota Press Council is consideration and processing of grievances against the Press and the editors and employees of the Press. The Council will undertake to hear, consider and adjust grievances after determining the essential facts of any controversy through hearings and any necessary investigations. In order to function effectively and fairly it is essential that a separate Grievance Committee be created and that operating procedures be established for the Committee. While a complete set of procedural rules must be provided for those instances where proper consideration of the grievance will require application of a full range of procedural rules, it is expected that the vast majority of grievances will not require such formal handling. For example, while due process rights such as the right of counsel are provided, it is expected that the parties will seek to have their attorneys directly involved only on very rare occasions in the processing of a grievance. The nature of the Council's function is such that informality of the proceedings is beneficial and formality at every stage will be discouraged.

While the composition of the Grievance Committee is not properly a subject for inclusion in these procedural rules, these rules are based upon the expectation that the Grievance Committee will be structured to directly reflect the same composition of public and professional interests as are reflected in the membership of the Press Council.

As used in these procedural rules the following terms shall be considered technical terms and to have the following meaning:

Press. Newspapers of general circulation in the state of Minnesota

Newspaper. The particular newspaper against whom a complaint or grievance has been made

Complainant. A person or organization who has or makes a grievance against a newspaper

I. Instituting or Commencing Grievances—

A. *Exhaustion of local remedies. No grievance should be processed unless the matter has first been presented to the newspaper by the complainant.*

Comment. The purpose of the Press Council is primarily to encourage mutual understanding between the Press and the local citizenry. One of the simplest and most effective methods to insure mutual understanding is personal face to face discussion of problem areas and disputes among the persons involved. The discussion should involve the editor or publisher of the newspaper and the complainant directly. By this personal meeting imagined affronts and misunderstandings can often be cleared up. If personal discussion with the local editor is made first, it will give the editor an opportunity to understand the nature and extent of the complainant's concern, to be advised more clearly regarding matters that are occurring in his community, and to more precisely present the newspaper's position. If the newspaper agrees it is in error, it will be possible for immediate corrective action to be taken by the newspaper, including publishing corrections. If the matter is not an error of the newspaper, but arises through misunderstanding by the complainant of the function of the Press, perhaps discussion of professional standards and understanding of the problems of the Press will resolve the problem at that point. If nothing else, at least the parties will be introduced to each other and the areas of dispute acknowledged and recognized between them.

Each grievance shall be temporarily withheld from further processing until the grievance has been presented to the newspaper and the newspaper has been given an opportunity to discuss the matter with the complainant and for such time as may be reasonably necessary for the parties to take such corrective actions as either party may deem desirable.

B. *Grievances can be brought by individuals and private and public entities against a newspaper, but not against individual employees of the newspaper.*

Comment. The newspaper should be considered responsible for the conduct of all of its employees in terms of the newspaper's relationship to the public. Therefore the grievance should be directed against the newspaper even though the actual cause may arise from conduct by an individual editor, reporter, or other employee.

In those grievances where it appears that a reporter's or other employee's professional conduct is the primary source of the grievance, the reporter or employee involved should be personally informed of the grievance and given an opportunity to participate directly in the proceeding as though he were in fact a party to the proceeding. In no event, however, will the newspaper be relieved of its ultimate responsibility for the conduct of its employees or be permitted to have the grievance dropped as to it. At all times it must be recognized that it is the complainant's grievance that is the sole issue before the Grievance Committee.

C. *No grievance will be considered if legal action based on the same subject matter is pending against the newspaper or an individual journalist. A grievance will not be processed until the complainant waives any possible future civil action that he may have arising out of the grievance for matters occurring prior to the filing of the grievance.*

Comment. It would seem desirable for the Council not to be involved in grievances in which litigation is pending. In like measure, it would not be desirable for the Council to consider a matter when the same or related matter may ultimately be presented to a court as a part of a civil claim. If a complainant wishes to invoke the process of the Press Council, he should recognize his resort to the Press Council will be his exclusive remedy for all matters relating to the subject matter of the grievance. Waivers of civil actions, of course, should not be waivers of legal actions for future incidents of alleged misconduct or repetition of the matter involved in the pending complaint.

D. *A party filing a grievance should waive libel and slander claims against persons providing the Council with information, against members of the Council and against the Press for publication of information acquired by the Council during its investigation and hearing process, or included in the Council's report.*

Comment. Proceedings by the Press Council are not protected by statutory privilege. As such, the Council should undertake to provide protection to persons giving information to the Press Council and protection to members of the Council to encourage high level professional and citizen involvement in the Council activities. Waivers of libel and slander claims contribute some incentive for full and complete participation both by the public, Council members, and the Press.

E. *Grievances resolved by agreement between the complainant and the newspaper following its presentation to the newspaper should not be further processed and the matter should be dropped at that point. No formal record should be kept of the grievance thus resolved.*

Comment. If the matter is disposed of following the initial presentation of the grievance to the newspaper, it would seem that the adjustment is personal and between the parties. The Press Council should not review the adjustment or indicate any assent or dissent to the arrangement. Since no responsibility is taken for the action, a record should not be maintained for the details of the initial inquiry other than the fact that it has been disposed of by personal adjustment.

F. *Grievances to be further considered by the Council must be filed with the Council in written form.*

Comment. If the complainant has difficulty expressing his grievance in written form, members of the Council staff should be free to assist the complainant in this endeavor. Care should be taken by the staff to insure that the facts are accurately expressed and that the staff person does not improperly influence or suggest additional areas of concern to the complainant.

II. Grievance Processing—

A. *Upon receipt of a written grievance, a copy of the grievance must be sent to the newspaper with a request that the newspaper reply promptly to the grievance in writing setting forth the newspaper's contentions.*

Comment. Procedurally it is desirable that each party's formal position be reflected by written statements. Since a written grievance initiates the process, it would seem desirable to have the newspaper's response also in written form. By compelling a writing at an early stage, the parties are less free to change positions factually later on in the proceedings, but more importantly, the parties are forced to think through their positions more clearly. There is no prejudice to the newspaper if the newspaper refuses to cooperate with the Council at this stage and refuses to provide a written statement. The opportunity to make a statement is a privilege, not an obligation. A failure to respond does not indicate agreement with the facts asserted in the grievance. A right to participate personally in future hearings can be denied until a written response is made.

B. *The Grievance Committee will review each filed grievance. The committee may establish and adopt a procedure for processing grievances, including a method for a preliminary screening of grievances.*

Comment. The Grievance Committee should be responsible for determining the sufficiency of each filed grievance and for adopting its own policies with regard to the method of processing grievances best designed to insure proper processing. The Committee should be free to adopt a preliminary screening procedure if it desires. In like measure, the Committee should have the freedom to determine whether or not each grievance must be processed by the entire Committee as a preliminary matter. Once the Committee has experience in processing grievances, the Committee should be free to amend its internal procedures without the necessity of obtaining approval from the entire Press Council and requiring an amendment to these procedural rules.

C. *The Grievance Committee shall make a preliminary and informal fact investigation including discussions with the complainant, the newspaper, the newspaper's reporters or employees, and witnesses. The investigation may be conducted by a designated staff person or members of the Committee and can involve written communication as well as personal conferences or telephone communication.*

Comment. Preliminary informal fact investigation is desirable to verify the facts alleged in the grievance and in the response. The Committee should be free to adopt whatever method is most desirable in a particular case or type of case for determining accuracy of statements and resolving questions regarding the nature of the grievance. No formal investigation steps should be required other than those steps the Committee deems necessary to determine whether or not a grievance is factually meritorious.

D. *If the grievance should be dismissed after preliminary investigation, the Grievance Committee should so advise the Press Council and, if concurred in by the Press Council, copies of the dismissal will be transmitted in written form to the complainant and to the newspaper together with a brief statement explaining the reasons for the dismissal.*

E. *A record will be kept of all grievances and the disposition of the grievance, including letters of dismissals. A summary of the record will be sent to all Council members periodically for their information.*

F. *If the Grievance Committee decides further Committee action is necessary, a hearing time will be scheduled for the Committee to consider the evidence and hear witnesses presented by the parties. All parties will have the opportunity to appear in person before the Committee and give oral testimony. Non-party witnesses can be called and examined only in the discretion of the Committee. A right to cross examination and a right to counsel are available for both parties. Normally no transcript of the hearing will be made, but the Committee or any party shall have the privilege of preserving the evidence in any reasonable manner he chooses, such as the use of tape recordings, etc. At all times the desirability of informality and flexibility of the proceedings must be recognized.*

Comment. A hearing may be necessary for the Committee to get a true flavor of the dispute and to determine the credibility of persons giving evidence by observing their demeanor. Basic due process requirements of confrontation, cross-examination and counsel should be available if the parties desire to exercise those rights, but such use should be discouraged and should be the exception, not the rule. The British believe that this type of administrative proceedings should not involve due process procedural protection. In this country it is generally believed that better factual results will be obtained if due process requirements are available for those rare situations where they are needed, or for persons who would feel more comfortable if assisted by an attorney, or for persons who want to examine an adverse witness.

G. *Additional investigations can be made and additional evidence can be presented to the Committee after the hearing at the direction of the Committee.*

Comment. At the end of the hearing questions may still exist with regard to fact matters. The Committee should be able to obtain this information either by investigation or by additional hearings.

H. *The Grievance Committee by majority vote will make the Committee's decision on the matter and recommend corrective action if any is deemed desirable. If a grievance involves a matter of broad general policy or could involve more than the one newspaper grieved against, the grievance must be transmitted to the Press Council for deliberation with or without recommendation by the Grievance Committee.*

Comment. Certain grievances may involve matters of general policy that properly should be considered as policy questions by the entire Press Council. Such grievances must be considered and resolved by the Council, and the Grievance Committee is free to refer such a grievance to the Press Council at any stage of its proceeding whenever the Committee feels that such referral is proper.

III. Recommendations and Reports—

A. *Except for grievances involving matters of general policy covered under II, H, conclusions and recommendations of the Grievance Committee will be transmitted to each of the parties in writing. Each party will be given a period of ten days to submit responses to the recommendations in writing before consideration of the recommendations by the Press Council.*

Comment. It would seem desirable that each party be advised of the intended report before public release of the recommendations of the Grievance Committee. If errors are made factually or legally the parties will have an opportunity to correct such errors.

B. *All recommendations of the Grievance Committee will be transmitted to the Press Council for its consideration.*

Comment. The recommendation of the Grievance Committee and the parties' response thereto should be sent to all members of the Press Council prior to the Council meeting.

C. *The Press Council will consider the recommendation of the Grievance Committee, and by majority of the Press Council members voting on the question can accept, reject, or amend the recommendation, or it can return the grievance to the Committee for further processing. After final action by the Press Council, the Press Council will make a written report of its action.*

D. *The report of the Press Council will be transmitted to the parties and to the news media for publication.*

IV. Appeal to the Council—

A. *Appeals from a dismissal by the Grievance Committee, or from a report of the Council in grievances where the parties have not previously appeared before the Council, will be permitted only at the discretion of the Press Council.*

Comment. An automatic appeal with an extended hearing by the entire Council in each case would not be beneficial in terms of preserving Grievance Committee integrity or in permitting the Council time to consider its other functions. Appeals involving new fact hearings should be the exception, not the rule. No party has a right to a new fact hearing or to appear personally before the entire Council. Such matters should be discretionary with the Press Council.

B. *Such appeals to the Press Council, when granted, ordinarily shall not be hearings de novo, but in the discretion of the Council new evidence may be heard.*

C. *The Press Council's deliberations need not be public.*

D. *Following the Press Council's deliberations, its recommendations will be reported to each of the parties and to the Press in the form of a report and the report can be published.*

Constitution of the
British Press Council (1963)

Articles of Constitution of The Press Council approved by The Newspaper Proprietors Association Ltd., The Newspaper Society, Periodical Publishers Association Ltd., The Scottish Daily Newspaper Society, Scottish Newspaper Proprietors' Association, The Institute of Journalists, the National Union of Journalists, and The Guild of British Newspaper Editors hereinafter referred to as the constituent bodies.

I. *Foundation*—The Press Council, hereinafter called the Council, is voluntarily constituted on and from the first day of July 1953, in the designation "The General Council of the Press." The Council revokes that style and title on and from the first day of July 1963, but accepts responsibility for all acts performed by The General Council of the Press as though they had been done by The Press Council.

II. *Objects*—The objects of the Council are:

A. To preserve the established freedom of the British Press.
B. To maintain the character of the British Press in accordance with the highest professional and commercial standards.
C. To consider complaints about the conduct of the Press or the conduct of persons and organisations towards the Press; to deal with these complaints in whatever manner might seem practical and appropriate and record resultant action.

D. To keep under review developments likely to restrict the supply of information of public interest and importance.

E. To report publicly on developments that may tend towards greater concentration or monopoly in the Press (including changes in ownership, control and growth of Press undertakings) and to publish statistical information relating thereto.

F. To make representations on appropriate occasions to the Government, organs of the United Nations and to Press organisations abroad.

G. To publish periodical reports recording the Council's work and to review, from time to time, developments in the Press and the factors affecting them.

III. *Membership*—The Council shall consist of:

A. A Chairman who shall be a person otherwise unconnected with the Press.

B. Twenty members nominated by the following bodies in the proportions indicated:

The Newspaper Proprietors Association Ltd. 5

    At least two of whom shall be editorial—as distinct from managerial—nominees

The Newspaper Society 3

    At least one of whom shall be an editorial nominee.

Periodical Publishers Association Ltd., including one editorial nominee 2

The Scottish Daily Newspaper Society 1

Scottish Newspaper Proprietors' Association 1

The Guild of British Newspaper Editors 2

The National Union of Journalists 4

The Institute of Journalists 2

C. Representatives of the Public who shall not exceed 20 percent of the Council's total membership entitled to vote 5

IV. *Methods of Appointment*—

A. The Chairman shall be invited to accept office on such terms as shall be agreed mutually by him and the Council.

B. Members nominated within the provisions of Clause III, B shall be persons who, at the time of appointment, are full-time directors of newspapers, periodicals, news agencies supplying a daily service of news to newspapers in Great Britain and/or overseas OR full-time editorial or managerial employees on the staffs of such organisations. Editorial qualification shall extend to include also full-time professional freelance journalists regularly engaged in supplying news and/or articles to recognised newspapers, periodicals or news agencies. A member ceasing to be so qualified shall notify the secretary or acting secretary of the Council in writing within one calendar month and his membership shall terminate within three calendar months.

C. Representatives of the Public co-opted to the Council shall be chosen by the Chairman and other members of the Council in consultation. These representatives shall rank equal with members nominated by the constituent bodies in the rights, privileges and duties inherent in membership of the Council other than qualification for election to the vice-chairmanship.

V. *Retirement*—On nomination to the Council a person shall be entitled to membership for three consecutive years. At the end of this period the nominee, if he is qualified, shall be eligible for reelection. On first appointment of the group of members specified in Clause III, B seven shall serve for only one year before retirement and a further seven for an initial period of two years. These members shall be decided by lot. They will be eligible for reelection and thereafter the normal period of their membership of the Council and that of their successors shall be three years. On first appointment of the group of members specified in Clause III, C one shall retire at the end of the first year of service and a further two at the end of two years' membership in similar manner and conditions.

VI. *Casual Vacancies*—A person filling a casual vacancy shall be appointed to membership in like manner to that by which the person whose vacancy he fills was appointed. On initial appointment he shall retain membership only for the unexpired portion of the period which remained to the person whose place in the Council he takes.

VII. *Procedure*—The Council is empowered by the constituent bodies to regulate and control all its procedure and action for the furtherance and attainment of the objects defined in Clause II hereof as the Council may decide. The Chairman and members shall each be entitled to cast one vote in any matter decided by them on a show of hands or by ballot, but if a division should result in an equal number of votes being cast for and against a motion the Chairman shall be entitled to exercise a casting vote.

VIII. *Quorum*—A quorum at a Council meeting shall be 13 members.

IX. *Vice-Chairman*—At its first meeting following the thirtieth day of June in each and every year the Council shall appoint from its members nominated under the provisions of Clause III, B a Vice-Chairman, who shall hold office until the first meeting of the Council in the following financial year and subject to possession of qualification, shall then be eligible for reelection. Nominations in writing, duly proposed and seconded, with the written consent of the nominee, must be submitted to the secretary not later than fourteen days before the meeting of the Council at which the election is to take place. In the absence of written nomination, oral nomination may be made at the appropriate meeting of the Council. If no nomination is made, the existing holder of the office shall be declared to have been reelected. In the absence of the Chairman the Vice-Chairman shall preside at Council meetings and he shall fulfill all the functions of the Chairman should that office be not occupied.

X. *Meetings*—Meetings shall be held at least five times a year. The Chairman is empowered to call a special meeting, if, in his opinion, the business to be transacted warrants this action. A special meeting shall be convened by the secretary on the requisition of not fewer than eight members. Such requisition shall be addressed to the secretary at the office of the Council for the time being. Not less than seven days' notice shall be given in writing of any meeting of the Council unless members agree to accept shorter notice.

XI. *Committees*—The Council shall have power to appoint committees of its members for the discharge of such duties as shall be specified. A committee shall not have executive authority unless this is expressly delegated to it by the Council. At the last Council meeting preceding the thirtieth day of June each year the Chairman and Vice-Chairman shall submit to the Council for its approval a list of members willing to serve on committees. Members of committees shall hold office from the date on which the list in which they are named is approved or the first day of July, whichever is the later, until the date on which their successors similarly take office. Upon the occurrence of one or more casual vacancies in the membership of a committee the Chairman and the Vice-Chairman may, at their discretion, submit to the Council for its approval the names of members willing to fill the vacancies and such members shall hold office on like terms as those whom they replace. Each committee shall appoint a Chairman from amongst its members. The Council Chairman and Vice-Chairman shall be ex officio members of all committees.

XII. *Notices*—Notice of meetings shall be sent to members of the Council at the addresses indicated by them to the secretary. Accidental omission to notify any of the said persons or nonreceipt by any of them of such notice shall not invalidate the proceedings of the meeting to which the notice relates.

XIII. *Finance*—The monetary expenditure of the Council shall be met by annual subscriptions payable by the constituent bodies as set out in the Schedule hereto. No variation in these amounts shall be made without the prior written consent of the constituent bodies. Subscriptions shall be payable on the first day of July in each year.

All cheques issued in the name of the Council shall be signed by any two of the following persons: The Chairman, the Vice-Chairman, the secretary, the assistant secretary and any other specially designated members of the Council.

XIV. *Travelling Expenses*—A member attending a meeting of the Council or of any of its committees shall be entitled to receive his first-class return railway fare from the funds of the Council.

XV. *Subsistence Allowances*—Members of the Council appointed under Clause III, C shall be entitled to receive from Council funds subsistence expenses incurred in attending council and/or committee meetings in accordance with rates to be fixed by the Council from time to time.

XVI. *Dissolution*—The Council may at any time terminate its existence if it appears to the members that the Council's voluntary nature and independence are threatened. A resolution to dissolve the Council, to be binding, must be passed by a two-thirds majority of its members present and voting at a meeting specially called for the purpose, which two-thirds majority shall be not less than a simple majority of the membership of the Council. Not less than twenty-one days' notice shall be given of any such meeting and this shall give particulars of the purpose for which the meeting is called. The Council shall notify secretaries of the constituent bodies of such meeting at the time it summons members.

XVII. *Alteration of Constitution*—Alteration of these Articles of Constitution shall require the approval of a two-thirds majority of the members present and voting at a meeting, which two-thirds majority shall be not less than a simple majority of the membership of the Council. No alteration shall be effective unless at least 28 days' notice of a proposed alteration shall have been given to Council members and secretaries of the constituent bodies.

XVIII. *Staff*—The secretarial and administrative work of the Council shall be carried out by an appointed secretary and a staff engaged for the purpose on terms and conditions decided by the Council from time to time.

XIX. *Revocation of Previous Articles of Constitution*— These Articles of Constitution shall have effect on and from the first day of July 1963. They supersede the original Articles of Constitution, dated the first day of July 1953, as amended in January 1959, and again in the financial year 1961-62 which are hereby revoked by resolution of the General Council of the Press this eighteenth day of June 1963.

Organization of the
Ontario Press Council

I. *Purpose*—Objects of the Ontario Press Council are:
A. To preserve the established freedom of the press.
B. To serve as a medium of understanding between the public and the press.
C. To encourage the highest ethical, professional, and commercial standards of journalism.
D. To consider complaints from the public about the conduct of the press in the gathering and publication of news, opinion and advertising; to consider complaints from members of the press about the conduct of individuals and organizations toward the press; and to report publicly on action taken.
E. To review and report on attempts to restrict access to information of public interest.
F. To make representations to governments and other bodies on matters relating to the objects of the Ontario Press Council.
G. To publish periodic reports recording the work of the Council.
II. *Membership*—
A. The Ontario Press Council shall have 21 members. Among the members shall be:
1. A chairman, who shall be appointed by the member newspapers.

2. Ten members who are officers or employees of the member newspapers and who shall be appointed by the member newspapers and who shall include editorial and business representatives.

3. Ten members not professionally associated with the media, who should be broadly representative of the communities in which member newspapers are published, and who shall be appointed by the chairman and the ten professional members.

4. Membership in the Council does not in itself confer on a member the right to a seat on the Council.

B. Appointments to the Council shall be for a one-year term but may be renewed for an additional term or terms.

III. *Procedure*—The Ontario Press Council shall establish its own rules and regulations subject to the following requirements:

A. The Council will meet at least three times a year.

B. A quorum shall be 13 members present in person, including the chairman.

C. Meetings of the Council shall be held in private.

D. All matters brought before the Council shall be in writing.

E. The Council may hear and question witnesses, but no complainant or other witness may be represented by counsel.

F. No complaint concerning a member newspaper shall be heard by the Council unless the complainant has given the newspaper an opportunity to satisfy the complaint. Any complaint brought before the Council shall include evidence of efforts to obtain redress directly from the newspaper.

G. The Council may decide not to consider a complaint if the complaint has not been received within six months after the occurrence of the matter complained of.

H. Every complainant shall sign a waiver agreeing not to take legal action on any complaint heard by the Council on which the Council makes a finding.

I. If a complaint is received concerning an Ontario newspaper which is not a member newspaper, the complaint shall be forwarded to the newspaper involved. If the newspaper chooses to have such a complaint dealt with, the Council will hear it. Otherwise the Council will report that the newspaper chose not to have the complaint heard.

J. The Council may establish a Complaints Committee to consider evidence and find upon the facts of a complaint,

88

and to report its findings to the Council for action by the Council.

IV. *Member Newspapers—*

A. Any daily newspaper published in Ontario is eligible to become a member of the Ontario Press Council.

B. Member newspapers shall have these responsibilities:

   1. To establish the Ontario Press Council; to appoint a chairman and 10 members representing the member newspapers, who shall in turn appoint 10 members representative of the public; to appoint an executive secretary.

   2. To receive from the Council by October 1 in each calendar year a proposed budget for the following calendar year for the operations of the Council and to approve the proposed budget, or modify it in consultation with the chairman and the executive secretary.

   3. To underwrite the operation of the Council. Each member newspaper shall contribute in the proportion of its circulation to the total circulation of all member newspapers, based on the latest publishers' six-month statements. Operating costs of the Council will include an honorarium for the chairman, an honorarium for each member of the Council representative of the public, the salary and necessary expenses of the executive secretary, and normal travel expenses of Council members attending meetings of the Council or otherwise occupied in business of the Council.

C. Member newspapers agree to publish all conclusions of the Council involving their newspaper, and whenever practical all other reports and conclusions of the Council.

D. Member newspapers may withdraw from the Council upon one year's notice.

V. *Changes to Organization of the Ontario Press Council—*
This organization of the Ontario Press Council may be changed upon a two-thirds vote of all Council members, if also approved by member newspapers.